Instructional Innovation+

Dedication

This book is dedicated to collaborative teaching teams everywhere who tirelessly engage in continuous self and collective improvement and have positive impacts on themselves, their students, colleagues, and educational institutions.

Instructional Innovation+

Cultivating Teaching Teams Through Action Research

Jorge Valenzuela

With contributions by

Serbrenia Sims,

Drew Hirshon,

Laurel Byrd, and Sara Leone

CORWIN

FOR INFORMATION:

Corwin
A SAGE Company
2455 Teller Road
Thousand Oaks, California 91320
(800) 233-9936
www.corwin.com

SAGE Publications Ltd.
1 Oliver's Yard
55 City Road
London EC1Y 1SP
United Kingdom

SAGE Publications India Pvt. Ltd.
Unit No 323-333, Third Floor, F-Block
International Trade Tower Nehru Place
New Delhi 110 019
India

SAGE Publications Asia-Pacific Pte. Ltd.
18 Cross Street #10-10/11/12
China Square Central
Singapore 048423

Vice President and Editorial Director: Monica Eckman
Senior Publisher: Jessica Allan
Senior Content Development Editor: Mia Rodriguez
Senior Editorial Assistant: Natalie Delpino
Project Editor: Amy Schroller
Copy Editor: Melinda Masson
Typesetter: C&M Digitals (P) Ltd.
Proofreader: Rae-Ann Goodwin
Cover Designer: Scott Van Atta
Marketing Manager: Olivia Bartlett

Printed and bound by CPI Group (UK) Ltd, Croydon, CR0 4YY

Library of Congress Cataloging-in-Publication Data

Names: Valenzuela, Jorge (Engineering teacher) author.

Title: Instructional innovation+ : cultivating teaching teams through action research / Jorge Valenzuela.

Description: Thousand Oaks, California : Corwin, [2025] | Includes bibliographical references.

Identifiers: LCCN 2024058626 | ISBN 9781071985014 (paperback) | ISBN 9781071985021 (epub) | ISBN 9781071985038 (epub) | ISBN 9781071985045 (pdf)

Subjects: LCSH: Action research in education. | Teaching teams. | Instructional systems—Design. | Educational technology.

Classification: LCC LB1028.24 .V33 2025 | DDC 370.72—dc23/eng/20250317
LC record available at https://lccn.loc.gov/2024058626

This book is printed on acid-free paper.

25 26 27 28 29 10 9 8 7 6 5 4 3 2 1

Contents

Please visit the companion website at
https://companion.corwin.com/courses/InstructionalInnovation+
to access the following contents:

- **Appendix A: Tools and Templates** as downloadable pages
- **Appendix B: Additional Resources for Instructional Innovation** listing links to professional development, books, websites and blogs, and podcasts

Acknowledgments

I want to thank God for grace and faith, my parents, Mariam, Anisa, Daniel, Graham, Theo, and my Goddaughter Jemma Deskins.

I express my deepest gratitude to my team and dear friends Tobias, Toni, and Majesty Reason, Steven Brown, and James Autry for their support and unconditional regard throughout my writing process.

Thank you to Tom Berger, Marva Hinton, Aaron Monroe, Tammi Ward, Dr. Troy Whalen, Sara Leone, Dr. Serbrenia Sims, Jeannine Freeman, Diana Fingal, ISTE, Richmond Public Schools, Victoria Oakley, Douglas Rife, Lauren Ware, Jamila Loving, Josh Tovar, Dr. Mickey Kosloski, Dr. Petros Katsioloudis, and Drew Hirshon for collaborating with me and contributing to my professional growth.

I am also grateful for the support of Corwin, Sonja Hollins-Alexander, Chris Devling, Monica Eckman, Amy Schroller, Melinda Masson, the schools I partner with, and my terrific editor, Jessica Allan.

The development of the instructional innovation models and practices described in this book was made possible by the invaluable contributions of the instructional leaders and hundreds of educators I collaborated with while coaching these topics through numerous workshops and data collections from 2007 to the present.

A Very Special Acknowledgment

It is common knowledge that no one succeeds alone, so I must include this separate acknowledgment for Sonja Hollins-Alexander. She saw potential in me, provided me with opportunities, and encouraged me to collaborate with others. Thank you for believing in me, Sonja! You've made a difference in my professional life.

Important Mentions

Instructional innovation through collaborative teams encompasses incredibly diverse and far-ranging topics and pedagogies to the extent that achieving a deep understanding necessitates learning from multiple individuals. I want to express my gratitude and acknowledgment to the following scholars and entities for their outstanding contributions to these areas and for their impact on me: the late Richard and Rebecca DuFour, Robert Eaker, Thomas W. Many, Shirley M. Hord, Mike Mattos, Dr. Anthony Muhammad, Luis Cruz, John Hattie, Robert Marzano, Nancy Frey, Dave Nagel, Douglas Fisher, Toni Faddis, Aida Allen-Rotell, Principal Kafele, and countless others.

About the Author

Jorge Valenzuela, PhD, is a highly sought-after and well-regarded performance and education coach, author, and speaker at Lifelong Learning Defined. Dr. Valenzuela got his start in education and has helped countless educators improve their instructional leadership and teaching skills. He specializes in emphasizing instructional innovation through action research and is a trusted deliverer of reputable professional training in collaborative team building, core instruction, project-based learning (PBL), STEM pathways, entrepreneurship, and life skills integration across the curriculum. Dr. Valenzuela is a faculty member at Old Dominion University. He partners with Corwin to provide professional development and ongoing support to schools and teaching teams in instructional innovation methodologies and innovative teaching approaches, such as PBL. He has authored several books and is the *Lifelong Learning Defined* podcast host.

Introduction

The Importance of Systems and Strategies: Lessons From Sports for Teaching Teams

Let's make teaching fun again and begin by imagining a group of friends who love basketball, baseball, football, or any other team sport. They get together daily (sometimes even on weekends) because they love the sport and their time together. They are all excellent players with varying running, throwing, and shooting talent. However, they don't have a system or playbook to outline their teamwork. They've played together and been friends for years, and they always have fun. They have even played against other novices and were victorious many times because of their talent—so they don't give any thought to not having a teamwork system. But, one day, another team possessing lesser talent and abilities challenged them to play.

This opposing team had an excellent system for collaboration and a set of plays for a given number of situations they could rely upon because they had previously rehearsed and implemented them. Who do you think won the game? It wasn't close—the challengers dominated the friends. In sports, teams' primary objective is to work together to be successful (win). Teams who've fine-tuned a system and set of strategies will often beat others who solely rely on their passion and talent to win games. Of course, having strategy alone doesn't only make winners or dictate success, but it makes for better odds.

The principle of having a sound system and strategies doesn't just hold in sports—we believe the same philosophy applies in schools. Instructional leaders and teachers in their schools must have a system and playbook to become collaborative and cohesive teaching teams to transform student learning and success outcomes. The information in this book strives to provide you with the system components, such as frameworks and tools, so your teaching team can develop its own unique system and playbook. We want you to experience and reflect on our system, collect data, and then continuously tweak and adapt what works best for your school's team.

Setting Foundations: Defining Teaching Teams

To proceed, let's define this book's **who**, **what**, and **how**. The who are collaborative teaching teams, the what is instructional innovation, and the how is action research. In any given school, a teaching team comprises both the leaders responsible for supporting teaching and learning (e.g., the principal, assistant principal, instructional coaches, and lead teachers) and members of the teaching staff. A teaching team is a tandem of educators, including leaders and teachers, who cultivate team cohesion through continuous trust building, sharing ideas, and reflecting on how to impact ongoing improvement in teaching strategies and learning outcomes in their school (Kolleck et al., 2021).

There is scholarly interest and a growing body of research analyzing the dynamics of collaborative teaching teams, how they engage, and the impact of their work on the outcomes they set for their schools (Kolleck, 2019; Kolleck et al., 2021; Richter & Pant, 2016; Schuster et al., 2021). In schools with a large staff, multiple teaching teams may consist of individual grade levels sharing common students. Schools with fewer staff may have one teaching team supporting the entire staff. We do not advocate for one approach of team building over another. Considering logistics and preferences in school buildings, teaching teams should choose the best way to achieve their academic and instructional goals. Here are four questions to help promote reflection and consideration as the team decides:

1. What are the needs of our staff?
2. Logistically, which approach works best for us?
3. What are the pros and cons of each approach?
4. What are the preferences of our team members?

With this solid understanding of who teaching teams are, we can now discuss instructional innovation (what teaching teams do) and its implementation through action research (how they do it).

Instructional Innovation in Education: An Ongoing Systematic and Data-Driven Process

COVID-19 has decimated instruction in many school systems across the United States (Kuhfeld, Soland, Lewis, & Morton, 2022), and although the pandemic is in the past, realigning educational strategies and student outcomes is challenging for many schools (Kirtman & Knight-Burney, 2023). Seasoned instructional leaders know instruction must continuously be closely monitored and improved in schools.

Though not easy, instructional innovation involves developing and implementing new instructional methodologies and strategies (including technology) to enhance student learning outcomes (Mumford et al., 2017). To implement sustainable instructional innovation, instructional leaders and school-based teaching teams should establish and rely on a systematic and data-driven action research approach informed by empirical evidence.

Action research is an investigation method teachers can employ to solve problems and improve professional practices in their schools and classrooms. Action research involves structured observations and data collection that practitioner-researchers use in reflection, decision making, and adapting and developing more effective classroom strategies (Mertler, 2021; Parsons & Brown, 2002). This book provides processes and a systematic action research approach to achieve instructional innovation and guide teaching teams in addressing their instructional problems by analyzing the obtained data.

The first few attempts by your teaching team to work through many of these processes may be clunky and time-consuming. Fret not; it gets easier with time. Because action research for school transformation is ongoing, you and your team will get better through repetition.

With this book, I aim to help teaching teams bridge the gap between high-yielding strategies and student achievement by making instructional innovation practical. As the author, my primary goal is to help guide your school through the intricate phases essential for this vital undertaking. Consider these necessary steps to ensure teachers' satisfaction and students' academic success.

Drawing on our collective expertise encompassing various educational roles—from superintendents, directors, and principals to instructional specialists and coaches—this book offers a multifaceted perspective that can help address the nuanced challenges educators face in diverse school settings. Providing teaching teams with a systematic and data-driven approach to improving instructional problems, our book encourages a focus on teamwork, assists in identifying classroom needs, and offers guidance for initiating improvements and utilizing metrics to enhance teaching practices.

Teacher Retention and Attrition Rates in Education: Hindrance to Instructional Innovation

Instructional innovation through action research is an ongoing, never-ending process in schools, and seasoned teaching team members willing to be both practitioners and researchers for the long haul are in demand. In recent years, the teaching profession has encountered challenges stemming from teacher shortages and an influx of nontraditional entrants, such as career switchers and teachers entering the profession during the pandemic, resulting in a disconnect between research-informed teaching practices and innovative instruction (American University School of Education, 2022).

Teacher retention has already been a pressing concern for some in education (Carver-Thomas & Darling-Hammond, 2017). It has really become heightened in recent years following the pandemic (Bryant et al., 2023). In 2020, attrition rates were higher than in previous years. Here is a breakdown of the trends since then (Bryant et al., 2023):

- Separations of education workers increased by 20 percent from 2019 to 2020.
- There was a 17 percent rise in separations from 2021 to 2022, and notably 64 percent were due to resignations.

Unfortunately, attrition due to quitting is on the rise in education, and improvements soon are not looking good, dampening schools' efforts to engage members of their teaching staff in meaningful instructional innovation. Of the teachers surveyed, 38 percent of those aged 25 to 34 reported planning to leave, compared with about 30 percent of their older counterparts (Bryant et al., 2023). This imbalance across age groups could severely lessen the educator workforce in the coming years. Explaining these complex realities in our book introduction is not meant to dishearten readers. Instead, it is intended to spotlight what prevents instructional innovation in schools, along with recommendations for working toward setting the stage for it and ensuring sustainability.

As teaching teams and school leaders know, having a seasoned and reliable teaching staff is more than just having the bodies required for instructional innovation efforts. At-risk and vulnerable students need consistent teachers, and many are suffering and will continue to suffer from attrition and mass exodus. The inability to retain good teachers ultimately sets many students back academically due to inconsistency in cultivating high-quality instruction. Notably, students of color in high-poverty school districts tend to be the most impacted by higher turnover and teacher vacancies (Bryant et al., 2023). This is one of the reasons why there is so much emphasis on building collaborative teams and providing effective feedback to teachers in Part I of this book. It is essential to try to retain the presence of the folks who youth desperately need.

The Processes Outlined in This Book and Outcomes for Teaching Teams

Our book outlines two critical paths to success in instructional innovation. The first path is a flexible framework meant to equip teaching teams with essential collaborative team-building and feedback protocols to cultivate confident teachers. Unifying the path to instructional innovation, we lay the groundwork with team building through co-creating shared agreements, core instruction, instructional alignment, and a practical teaching structure, making differentiation strategies feasible for educators of varied experiences.

Teams that are unsure if they need to do all of the level-setting work and are anxious to get to the instructional innovation process in Part II should honestly ask themselves the following questions:

1. What are the ingredients that comprise an effective and cohesive teaching team, and how well do we collaborate with others?
2. Do we know the critical components of curriculum and instruction development and implementation? How well can we teach it to our new teachers and administrators?
3. How is our school currently better because of our efforts?
4. Are we a difference maker for the staff and students we serve?

If any of your team's responses show the need to make the necessary improvements outlined in Part I of this book, there is no shame in taking time to ensure your team develops the required level of cohesion for success at your school.

Once your teaching team and core instruction are cohesive, the second path leads your teaching team through a five-step action research approach to instructional innovation. Adapting this process aids teams in comprehending the necessary steps and the chronological order for design and implementation, ensuring the long-term sustainability of your team's instructional innovation.

Implementing these two approaches, following the steps detailed in the chapters of this book, can be essential to your teaching team's journey toward achieving profound and sustained long-term outcomes, such as the following:

- Establish a system for instructional innovation and working knowledge of the action research process using a collaborative approach in schools.
- Establish a district- and/or schoolwide instructional model that clearly identifies the components of core instruction for administrators and teachers.
- Develop site-based shared agreements that outline how instructional teams will collaborate and work together.
- Follow a structured five-step action research approach to sustainable instructional innovation.
- Conduct instructional rounds through learning walks to assess which areas of core instruction need improving.
- Gain a clear understanding of the required steps for designing and implementing specific interventions by conducting data debriefs.
- Establish milestones to create a chronological order for the instructional innovation journey specific to each school.

- Establish and implement protocols for providing teachers with effective feedback supporting their professional growth and development in all facets of instruction.
- Develop and administer mixed-method survey instruments to evaluate professional development interventions for a data-driven approach.

Ultimately, this book aims to help teaching teams achieve successful outcomes regarding positive school culture, teacher satisfaction, and student academic success through a structured and well-informed approach to instructional innovation.

Our Instructional Innovation Stories and Expertise

In this section and throughout the chapters in this book, I share compelling narratives from my and the contributors' diverse experiences within various school systems. These stories spotlight the critical role of the prescribed methods for instructional innovation in shaping our career successes. Each narrative offers insights and practical lessons learned from implementing this book's prescribed strategies, providing you, the reader, with authentic real-world examples of how these strategies can be effectively applied in different educational settings.

Jorge (Author)

Sadly, I was not introduced to instructional innovation throughout my five years in the classroom from 2003 to 2007. To my credit, I was passionate about the science, technology, engineering, and mathematics (STEM) content I taught, and developed a great rapport with students and my supervisors. I managed students well and often received the ones other teachers did not want in their elective classes.

Displaying a positive demeanor, strong work ethic, and high acumen for what my bosses required, as well as fostering positive relationships with others, unknowingly propelled me to a central office position as an instructional specialist in the city of Richmond, Virginia, in the summer of 2007. It was there that I was thrust into the thick of instructional innovation. My new environment was fast-paced, and I had a lot to learn in order to keep up with the vast knowledge and experience of my colleagues. I also wanted to make valuable contributions to the team's work. I did not want anyone to think I didn't deserve to be in my new role.

At the time, Richmond Public Schools (RPS) had strong instructional leaders. Drs. Deborah Jewell-Sherman and Yvonne Brandon led the helm and were moving what once was a struggling school system toward full accreditation of 50 schools. Our director of curriculum and instruction, Victoria Oakley, ensured each instructional specialist participated in quarterly instructional rounds and yearly audits in each school. Regardless of the content area each specialist supervised, we were responsible for learning core instruction, the four core content areas, and the extended core (electives) offering of the school system.

Visiting classrooms and refining my instructional innovation through action research approaches consistently for three years taught me to support teachers in planning and facilitating instruction in any content area. It also helped me find the balance between being a practitioner-researcher and showing others how to do the same. Given that we had a vibrant and dynamic team assisting schools, RPS saw results and became fully accredited in 2010 (Jenks, 2010).

Unfortunately, the success we experienced in those golden years was halted after administrations changed along with the approach to instructional innovation. The first thing to go was visiting classrooms; the system has yet to recover. In 2014, I joined the Buck Institute for Education (BIE) and became a master teacher. BIE began sending me to facilitate workshops for educators in K–16 institutions, and I learned education in several contexts (rural, inner-city, high-performing, low-performing, etc.).

Coupling my know-how of visiting classrooms to personalize teacher development I learned at RPS, this new experience of expert teaching provided me the know-how for helping superintendents and school leaders lead instructional innovation efforts in various school systems throughout the United States. I opened my own education consulting firm, Lifelong Learning Defined, in 2017 and have become a trusted and strategic thought partner for other instructional leaders.

These various experiences have taught me that instructional innovation requires a working understanding of school-based action research, partnerships with stakeholders, intentionality for using tools and resources, and a dedicated teaching team willing to participate in a data-driven action research process.

Serbrenia (Contributor)

I began my educational career in Virginia as a Williamsburg-James City County Public Schools teacher and later became the director of accountability, grants, and program evaluation. Early on, I learned the importance of instructional innovation and developing data-driven processes throughout my professional decision making. Doing so always kept me on the cutting edge of the latest educational research and able to tackle new instructional challenges systematically. I later served as an assistant principal and principal at York County Public Schools. I served as a summer school principal there and worked with others to develop and implement Tier 2 and 3 interventions.

In 2007, I joined Surry County Public Schools, which needed help to meet state accreditation. I was the principal of Luther Porter Jackson Middle School. In 2009, I began working as the assistant superintendent for instruction and was eventually promoted to division superintendent in 2020. As a superintendent, I implemented instructional innovation through action research to strengthen collaboration among school teams and both internal and external stakeholders. Curriculum and instruction guided our ship and decisions in how we collaborated with others.

Additionally, my devotion to annual instructional audits and quarterly instructional rounds helped me stay informed about the needs of my diverse teaching staff and students. Remaining connected to classrooms through processes I developed with my teaching teams in schools resulted in full accreditation for several years, which I am very proud of. One of the hallmarks of our program was ensuring every educator in the system with an administrative license participated in instructional audits. This resulted in developing and sustaining a culture of collaboration and growing instructional leaders prepared to take instructional innovation to higher levels.

Drew (Contributor)

My educational path has been unique with many instructional innovation opportunities. As a first-year teacher in 2007, I was selected by the superintendent of my district to be a part of starting a new International Baccalaureate (IB) school. Through this experience I was introduced to inquiry-based learning, interdisciplinary learning, having a global context, focusing on critical thinking, and student-centered assessments. As a young educator, I was thrust into pedagogy that was challenging to implement. Through this initial journey in my career I was fortunate to have leadership who supported my growth through utilizing observation feedback cycles, which supported my open-mindedness to coaching and feedback as a young educator.

Several years later, I was offered the opportunity to move to a neighboring high school where I was given the opportunity to become the STEM/project-based learning (PBL) coordinator after the school received a Magnet Schools Assistance Program (MSAP) grant. This opportunity is what led me to developing my skills as an instructional coach and leader. Additionally, this is where I was introduced to the BIE and Gold Standard PBL. Through training and implementation at the high school level, I became an expert in facilitation of professional learning and facilitation of professional learning communities to support teacher growth.

Although I loved supporting teachers and leaders in implementation of instructional innovation, I had an opportunity to open a school with a focus on instructional innovation as the vision from the outset. I was part of a team that opened up one of the first project-based maker schools in southern Colorado as a teacher, then became the principal. This K–8 school was designed to provide students with an instructional model that allowed for divergent thinking, voice and choice, creativity, and opportunities to tackle authentic problems in the community and world. Not only were we able to create this vision and opportunity for the community, but students succeeded at high levels. In two short years we received the Colorado Governor's Distinguished Improvement Award for academic growth and achievement.

My goal has always been to have the greatest positive impact on education that I possibly can, so my next step was to support the district administrative position by becoming the assistant director of curriculum where I was in charge of new teacher induction, professional learning, and secondary education and career technical education (CTE). In this role I was able to lead instructional innovation through developing a culture of shared leadership and implementation of learning walks. In the two years I was in the position, all of the secondary schools were performance schools, and one of the middle schools received a National Blue Ribbon Schools designation, but the greatest data point that I saw was having the highest Teaching and Learning Conditions Colorado data that the district has ever seen.

Building a culture of psychological safety, teacher agency, and effective teacher collaboration has contributed to my team's success and is how I strive to lead. In my current position as director of magnet schools, I am working with others, including Jorge, to create those same systems to allow for instructional innovation.

Sara (Contributor)

Growing up, children are often posed with a simple question: What do you want to be when you grow up? Certainly, answers vary from child to child, year to year, and, in some cases, minute to minute. You want to be a lion tamer? Fantastic. An astronaut? Outstanding. A professional athlete or pop superstar? The sky's the limit. As adults, we encourage the dreams of the younger generation because Americans hold fast to the notion that anything is possible. In my case, from an early age, 5 to be exact, when filling in my All About Me poster in kindergarten, I clearly knew I wanted to be a teacher. Looking back, was it because I was influenced by my loving teacher? Perhaps to an extent, but really, in hindsight, I recognize it was a calling. To this day, I firmly believe people are born to be teachers, and I am fortunate to consider myself one of those lucky people.

Upon college graduation, I was eager and ready to take the educational field by storm, but little did I know that landing a job in teaching was more competitive than I thought. After a few interviews, I settled into my first teaching position; while it was not quite the placement I had envisioned, I had the opportunity to have my very own classroom with students. Then it dawned on me: I would have *my very own classroom* with *students*! As millions of questions raced through my brain, I questioned how I, as a 22-year-old, could educate children when I myself was barely an adult. Somehow, I did it, a day at a time, with guidance from veteran teachers and coffee—lots of coffee! Sure, mistakes were made, and I probably need to find those students from my first class and thank them for their patience and trust and for allowing me to learn to grow as a teacher. I only stayed at that school for one year before I found my forever home in my current district, where I have been for the last 20 years.

Quickly, I established myself as a competent teacher who used innovative strategies to make learning accessible for all students. As I grew more confident in my craft, I saw my role slowly shift from teacher to teacher leader. By leaning into this shift and embracing it, I entered into my master's program for administration. My impact in my classroom and on my grade-level team was fantastic, but I knew I could widen my sphere of influence if I moved into an administrative role. After 14 years of teaching in the district, I made the transition to administration, and I have never looked back. Starting as an associate principal, then assuming a short interim principal position, I finally landed as a director of curriculum and instruction, two years ago.

As an administrator now in the central office, I have the opportunity to view instruction from a global level. For me this is a tremendous responsibility as I select curricular resources, align instructional programming, and continually evaluate program effectiveness to ensure that every student leaves our district with the necessary skills to be successful in high school and beyond. With each decision related to instruction and curriculum, I consider how it impacts student learning. What has become tremendously clear to me is that strong curriculum alignment and instructional innovation are pivotal for students' academic success, and it is crucial that this endeavor is led and supported by the administration. Teachers are on the front line with students and always will be, but with thoughtful support, specific ongoing professional development, and visible engaged administrators, schools will continue to evolve to provide meaningful educational experiences for all students.

Laurel (Contributor)

My career in education began with a Spanish degree, a love of learning, and the need for a job. What has transpired has been a result of hard work, a commitment to learning and applying what I've learned, not settling for "just enough," and pivotal relationships. From my first job in a public school (which, by the way, started four days before students arrived) to this day, I cannot understate the critical need to surround myself with people who are like-minded! Those first two years I was mentored—more like carried—by excellent teachers and an administrator who coached me.

I moved to a rural district and completed the requisite few classes to get my license. As in most small school divisions, everyone wears multiple hats, and there are no such things as "curriculum specialists," "instructional coaches," and so on. So, when I used up the very limited tools in my toolbox, I started to hunt down research and resources on my own. Thus began this journey! At the heart of innovation is a desire to learn, grow, accept challenges, and not fear failures. During my growth as a professional, I very rarely received professional development or feedback that actually spurred positive change in my teaching practices. In small divisions, many leaders are the "jack of all trades," but instruction usually falls by the wayside.

This launched my desire to go into administration for several reasons. I realized that teachers are amazing people and, if the right conditions are created for them to feel safe, valued, and equipped, they will give 150 percent to quality instruction and care for students. Another reason is that I wanted to provide teachers with the challenge and expectation to know the research on great instruction—and use it! Take risks! Try something new without fear of penalty! As a middle school principal, I was able to introduce restorative practices, focus professional development on instruction, and create processes throughout the school to support student learning. Again, these initiatives were not brought by division leaders, but because I just knew that there were better ways to do things as a school leader, I went hunting for them!

Creating a safe climate, having feedback processes in place, establishing shared agreements, examining data, and progress monitoring goals: These are all systems that must be in place for innovation to occur. Through our work with Jorge, we were able to really articulate those. It was an empowering experience for all of us! Now that I am a middle/high school principal, these same principles and strategies are being used to get to know my educators and their instruction, create trusting relationships and teams, and push instruction to higher levels. Training teachers to embrace innovation is a huge goal that must be modeled by school leaders. It's worth it—not just for students but for the educators in the classrooms who need to feel valued and who should be learning and growing as professionals.

Who Should Read This Book

We wrote this book for collaborative teaching teams in schools and also for individuals responsible for supporting teachers and improving instruction in schools. Specifically, the following job titles, along with the roles we outline, would benefit from the guidance provided in this book:

- **Superintendents of instruction** oversee a portion or the entirety of a district's educational landscape and set the tone and direction for instructional innovation efforts and initiatives.
- **District-level administrators** work with superintendents of instruction to implement academic programs, instructional innovation efforts, and initiatives across multiple schools.
- **Principals and assistant principals** directly manage and support teachers in teaching and learning efforts in an individual school setting.
- **Curriculum specialists and instructional coaches** provide specialized expertise and guidance to educators in refining instructional design practices. Many travel across several schools to support many teachers.
- **Teacher leaders** play a pivotal role in fostering collaboration and disseminating best practices among their peers in the schools where they teach.
- **Professional development coordinators and educational consultants** contribute to instructional innovation by designing and delivering targeted training programs and resources.

- **Professional learning communities (PLCs)** are not a specific position. However, PLCs are collaborative teams of educators who regularly collaborate to improve teaching practice and student learning outcomes.
- **Important note about PLCs:** This book's instructional innovation and action research processes are independent of both Solution Tree's PLC and Corwin's PLC+ work. Instead, the information and resources in this book can complement PLCs seeking systematic approaches to action research.

These aforementioned individuals support and lead teachers and instructional teams to enhance educational outcomes in schools and districts. They are vital in executing sustainable instructional innovation and would benefit from an organized and informed approach toward achieving these goals and objectives.

How to Navigate This Book

This book is organized into two parts, each with four or more chapters. Part I (Chapters 1–4) establishes the groundwork for instructional innovation and team transformation. Through foundational chapters, it emphasizes the importance of shared agreements for cohesive team dynamics, the impact of constructive feedback on teacher retention and satisfaction, the essential elements of effective core instruction, and tools for aligning and facilitating instruction aligned with student learning goals and assessments. Chapters 1–4 each represent a step of the mind map introduced in Part I (see page 15). They are as follows.

- **Chapter 1, "Fostering Synergy: Creating Shared Agreements for Collaborative School Environments,"** focuses on building cohesive school-based teaching teams dedicated to synergizing instructional innovation efforts.
- **Chapter 2, "Empowering Teachers: Effective Strategies for Providing Feedback,"** explores strategies for differentiating timely feedback to boost teachers' confidence in teaching and address their instructional needs.
- **Chapter 3, "The Five Key Building Blocks of Effective Core Instruction,"** delves into the components comprising sound core instruction, aiding the teaching teams in compartmentalizing these foundational blocks.
- **Chapter 4, "Tools for Aligning Instruction and Assessment,"** focuses on aligning and mapping assessment-driven daily lessons, offering guidance in structuring expert facilitation for differentiated instruction.

Part II builds on the foundation in Part I by introducing a detailed action research model that school-based teaching teams can carry out in five steps, empowering team leaders to address instructional challenges using data. This model guides teams through crafting problem statements, conducting instructional rounds through classroom observations, goal setting, data analysis, and strategic professional development planning by setting practical milestones. Teaching teams implementing these steps can work collaboratively to address challenges impeding instruction, refine teaching practices, and mastermind meaningful improvements within their school settings. The chapters in Part II are as follows.

- **Chapter 5, "Step 1: Pinpointing Key Instructional Challenges and Problems of Practice,"** explores strategies for identifying and addressing critical instructional challenges within educational settings.
- **Chapter 6, "Step 2: Conducting Instructional Rounds Using Learning Walks,"** emphasizes the significance of conducting instructional rounds, particularly the use of learning walks, to observe current instruction and identify areas for improvement.
- **Chapter 7, "Step 3: Analyzing Learning Walk Data and Identifying Solutions Through Structured Data Debrief,"** guides teaching teams in effective action planning by discussing and analyzing data collected during learning walks, focusing on generating solutions and identifying barriers to addressing instructional challenges.
- **Chapter 8, "Step 4: Designing Data-Driven Professional Development Interventions for Solutions,"** focuses on creating personalized and integrated professional development (PD) interventions based on data analysis, prioritizing solutions, and categorizing PD interventions into strands and milestones.
- **Chapter 9, "Step 5: Implementing Data-Driven Professional Development,"** concentrates on implementing developed PD strands and milestones, emphasizing the collection of participant data to evaluate the effectiveness of interventions.

Finally, note that in many chapters, you will find important notes for readers featuring boxes highlighting unique concepts or strategy elements. Additionally, we aim to supplement and clarify the reader's understanding throughout the book and conclude each chapter with three individual reflective prompts and three for the team. The reflective prompts promote personal growth and facilitate meaningful discussion among team members. Each prompt addresses critical aspects of the content in each chapter. This book also provides access to downloadable additional resources in Appendices A (page 151) and B (online only). Finally, this book concludes with cited references and resources.

Part I

Unifying the Path to Instructional Innovation

Part I of this book, "Unifying the Path to Instructional Innovation," sets the stage for educational transformation through four foundational chapters that support the implementation of the Five-Step Instructional Innovation Model in Part II. The first chapter addresses the challenges district leaders and principals face in fostering cohesive teams, emphasizing the significance of shared agreements to create collaborative school environments. The second chapter focuses on providing constructive feedback to teachers, highlighting its impact on retention and job satisfaction. The third chapter explores the five essential elements of effective core instruction, while the fourth chapter delves into tools for aligning instruction and assessment. (See the following mind map representation of the elements for unifying the path to instructional innovation.) By combining these chapters, educators can cultivate collaborative teams, deliver valuable feedback, enhance core instruction, and align instruction with assessment, laying a solid groundwork for instructional innovation.

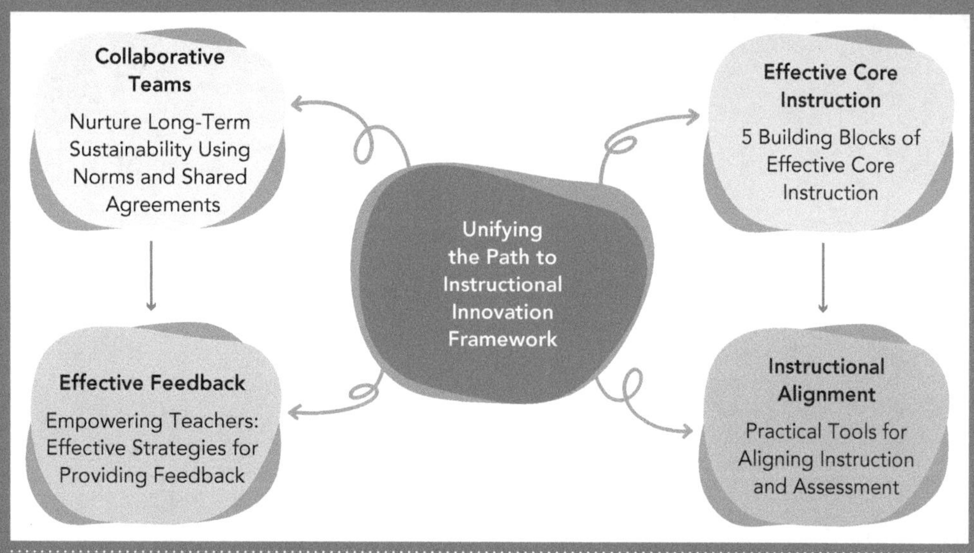

CHAPTER 1

Fostering Synergy

Creating Shared Agreements for Collaborative School Environments

This chapter starts us unifying the path toward instructional innovation. It discusses the difficulties system leaders and principals face when trying to create cohesive, productive, and happy teams among staff and faculty that focus on the well-being of students. Here, we, the author and contributors, stress the significance of establishing shared agreements or norms as a foundation for collaborative relationships in school environments. The forthcoming pages highlight the advantages of these agreements, such as more cohesive school teaching teams, the utilization of team members' abilities, the respect for diverse viewpoints, the attainment of clear organizational goals, and the creation of healthy frameworks for problem solving.

With decades of experience between us, we acknowledge that simply having shared agreements cannot resolve all school issues but can aid in successful problem solving. The chapter also recognizes the importance of taking time to understand the beliefs and motivations of resistant colleagues, building trust, and addressing past conflicts before beginning the process of creating shared agreements. It provides practical steps for starting the process, including setting basic agreements, reflecting on individual needs and deal-breakers, and discussing the desired culture.

Challenges and Opportunities: The Role of Shared Agreements in Teaching Team Environments

This book intends to guide your teaching teams in developing cohesion while engaging in instructional innovation as an ongoing process, first by unifying the path to instructional innovation in Part I and second by carrying out instructional innovation by engaging in action research in Part II. However, in this section, it's

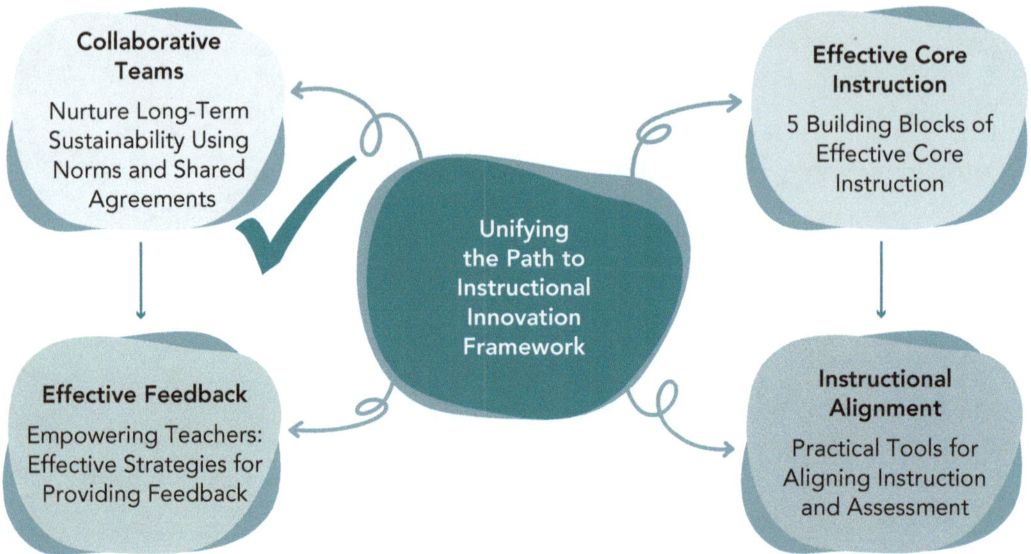

important to address some of the key concerns we encounter in the schools looking to begin building a cohesive teaching team by establishing shared agreements. The following are items that should be considered for fostering the togetherness required for building an effective teaching team.

One of the biggest challenges that district leaders, principals, and teaching team leaders face in today's schools is getting teaching teams on the same page to collaborate effectively. Addressing this challenge requires taking the steps to develop and support cohesive teams. This becomes even harder to achieve when morale is low and people are divided for many reasons. Recognizing these challenges is imperative by exploring and shedding light on the complexities preventing teaching teams from working together for student success.

Drawing from studies, the following bullet points elucidate key concerns teaching teams must consider regarding low educator morale and the factors contributing to divisions between people in schools. These findings underscore the importance of team and culture building, establishing shared agreements supported by scholarly insights, and teaching teams agreeing to tackle their school issues.

Contributors to Low Educator Morale:

- High levels of stress and burnout (Agyapong et al., 2023)
- Decreased job satisfaction and enthusiasm in the teaching profession (Toropova et al., 2021)
- Increased teacher turnover rates due to dissatisfaction (Toropova et al., 2021)
- Retaining experienced and effective educators (National Education Association, 2022)

- Teacher absenteeism and disengagement in the classroom (Red Rover, 2023)
- Teacher attrition and shortage (Lieberman, 2022; Will, 2022)
- Negative impacts on student learning outcomes (Kuhfeld, Soland, & Lewis, 2022; Kuhfeld, Soland, Lewis, & Morton, 2022; Lieberman, 2022)

Divisions in Schools:

- Lack of alignment among different stakeholders (teachers, administrators, parents, students) regarding educational goals (Sattar et al., 2022)
- Tensions and conflicts among educators, often stemming from differing teaching philosophies or strategies (Valente et al., 2020)
- Hierarchical divisions between administrators and teachers (Rinehart Kathawalla & Mehta, 2022)
- Differences in perspectives concerning curriculum, discipline, and educational priorities (Griffith & Tyner, 2019; Pak et al., 2020)
- Cultural or generational gaps among staff (Hansen & Quintero, 2019)
- Challenges in nurturing a collaborative and cohesive school culture (Keenan, 2017; Keenze-Wells, 2022)
- Impacts on student well-being and achievement resulting from divisions among adults in the school community (Sattar et al., 2022)

Navigating these educational challenges requires teaching teams to embrace growth and transformation and inspire the teachers they work with to do the same. In the following sections, we will delve into how some of these challenges impact the success of teaching teams, including how to address and navigate divisive colleagues. We will begin by providing essential items you and your colleagues must consider to foster highly functional, cohesive teams. We'll then expand our understanding by exploring the pivotal role shared agreements can play in developing and supporting collaborative teaching teams. Additionally, shared agreements can be leveraged to nurture a school culture dedicated to the well-being and success of both staff and students.

Fostering Cohesive Teaching Teams

For teaching teams to be effective in their instructional innovation and other efforts, they must always strive to be cohesive (Tutolo, 2017). This may be difficult to achieve in educational institutions where some colleagues resist and oppose change. Resistant colleagues can disrupt the organizational culture and climate and seriously impede instructional innovation efforts. When coaching teams, many ask if getting everyone to embrace change and the discomfort required for instructional innovation is truly possible. Our response is always that it requires a few extra steps, but it isn't impossible. Good practice has been studied enough for educators to find what practices have the most promise in their school context.

Research suggests (Hagger et al., 2014) that achieving group consensus is possible but requires a nuanced understanding of intrinsic motivations and their influences, such as collective teacher efficacy and cultural dynamics.

Fostering Collective Teacher Efficacy for Cohesive Teaching Teams

Here's why we believe team cohesion is possible. According to John Hattie (n.d.), collective teacher efficacy (CTE) is strongly correlated to student achievement and success and positive school culture. Efficacy is both the desire and belief in the ability to produce a desired effect. If the collective desired effect became creating strong team cohesion to ensure their students' success, teaching teams could eventually achieve it with time and adhering to sound practice. Based on the strong effects of CTE, we believe it can be a critical step in building a cohesive team. The same could be said about the effect of CTE on other desired team objectives—such as improving access to opportunities for students with fewer resources and improving reading comprehension in specific grade levels.

In addition to fostering their CTE, teaching teams need to understand how to cultivate cohesion among their members and their school's teaching staff. Some of the characteristics of team cohesiveness in the workplace are trust, conflict, commitment, accountability, and results, as defined by Patrick Lencioni (DiSC, n.d.). Before proceeding, let's break down what it means to be cohesive. The term *cohesive* is derived from *cohesion*, which means to stick or hold together firmly. In this book's context, cohesive teaching teams are united and collaborate effectively on the goals and objectives they set in their instructional innovation efforts at their school.

In subsequent chapters, teams will work together to establish a solid foundation for good core instruction and the action research methodology required for informed instructional innovation. As teams learn to engage in these processes, they will need to rely on each other to identify instructional problems and develop effective interventions and timelines. Helping to foster cohesion and interdependency within teaching teams is ongoing, and the purpose of working together to establish a set of norms and shared agreements is a first step in this chapter.

Creating a Supportive Environment: Understanding Culture and Climate

Supporting cohesive teaching teams requires a deep understanding of organizational culture and climate. Many teams we work with do not fully comprehend the difference between these two distinct concepts and often use them interchangeably. As per Professor Kent D. Peterson, school culture pertains to shared values, agreements and beliefs, everyday norms, and behaviors that make up the school's persona (Education World, n.d.; Muhammad, 2018).

Organizational climate is very different and refers to the team's prevailing atmosphere or mood, such as unity, morale, trust, and perceptions about the working dynamics (Hughes & Pickeral, 2013). Simply put, climate pertains to how the team feels, or temperature (warm, cold, windy, etc.), while culture relates to the team's everyday actions (Gruenert & Whitaker, 2015; Muhammad, 2018).

Teaching teams must comprehend these two concepts correctly and consider them when devising their shared agreements. To cultivate a collaborative culture, teaching teams should center some of their shared agreements on values, beliefs, and practices essential for nurturing adaptability, cohesion, and teamwork. To cultivate a positive school climate, teams must actively work toward ensuring everyone feels valued, respected, and supported. The shared agreements they create in the subsequent sections must include ways of addressing feelings of discomfort, challenges, and conflict within the team.

Another critical aspect of organizational culture teaching teams must consider is formal versus informal culture. According to Dr. Anthony Muhammad (2018),

> Organizational theorists agree that every organization has both a formal and informal structure. The formal organization consists of the organization's official arms. The informal organization consists of all covert alliances that develop as a result of interaction in the formal organization. These alliances are not officially sanctioned, and their members create their goals, so they are only governed by those who participate. They have no formal rules. An informal alliance's goals are generally not in alignment with those of the formal organization, which often makes the informal organization a threat to the formal organization's productivity and longevity (Pyöriä, 2007). Fundamentalists work very effectively in the informal organization. (pp. 89–90)

The informal culture should be addressed because even after establishing cohesion, teaching teams must also effectively engage the teachers they serve. How else can instructional innovation flourish in their educational setting? Furthermore, the staff members Muhammad (2018) refers to as "fundamentalists" are colleagues who resist and oppose change initiatives. Many resistant colleagues hold organizational power and, if left unchecked, are a significant roadblock to instructional innovation and any other form of meaningful transformation in schools.

Set Realistic Expectations About Your Teaching Teams' Shared Agreements

Before commencing with this strategy, every teaching team member should know that having a set of norms and shared agreements does not mean the team can solve every school issue—especially when tackling overly complicated ones where the teaching team cannot control all the factors. It is also important to consider that just because the team is fortunate to solve a major problem does not mean other challenges will not soon arise. On the bright side, the team will have experienced success in activating their shared norms and guidelines for navigating complex situations.

Collaboration with others in teaching teams requires a lot of trust, and establishing trust is not easy for everyone—especially for those who have felt let down in the past. Some of your teaching team members may find that some fence-mending must happen first. In that case, encourage parties to settle differences and offer mediation if required. Sometimes, working together to establish these guidelines can lead to heightened emotions. In heated moments, someone may break one or more of the agreements. That is OK. People are human—we are not a set of norms. When this happens, it is OK to table the discussion and return when agreements and collegiality can be upheld. In our collective experience we've seen team members who have not gotten along for years soften their stands after conversing on their differences and what's best for the school—leading to more empathetic agreements.

In schools facing organizational challenges, team members need to look out for one another, and solutions cannot come entirely from outside your school or district. The latest education trends, speakers, or books will only help if they know your workspace the way you and your staff do. Instead, use resources as helpful guides while establishing your team's shared agreements and rely on one another to lead with genuine empathy. Implement your agreements, collect relevant data, and refine your practices as you learn what works best for your school's teaching team.

Defining Shared Agreements

Shared agreements, also termed working agreements, community agreements, or shared expectations, are guidelines and norms that define how a group ideally wants to work together and what they wish to experience in their working environment (Haskell, 2013; Valenzuela, 2022a). Initially getting teaching team members on the same page about how they'll work together may be challenging for some teaching team leaders. Developing shared agreements within the scope of this book involves a process in which teaching team organizers facilitate the team's creation of agreements. These shared agreements serve as a pathway, providing willing team members with the open door to communicate and empathize appropriately and effectively with their team. The shared agreements are a tool that lies at the core of establishing a teaching team working environment and dynamic conducive to synergy.

The Benefits of Teaching Teams Creating Shared Agreements

Who wouldn't want a more agreeable work environment? Unfortunately, not everyone thinks alike, and sometimes, establishing a collaborative teaching team requires just as much time and effort as solving instructional problems. As therapist Vienna Pharaon sagely stated, "Behind every great relationship are difficult and uncomfortable conversations **we rarely get to see**. Great relationships don't just fall into our laps. They require people to move through their fears and insecurities and do the hard work to move wounds into healing" (quoted in Best Self, 2022). We, therefore, have to put in the work to get on the same page with our team members—and it works a lot better when everyone agrees to try. That is where shared agreements can help teaching teams.

Drawing from the author's vast and extensive experiences, educator teams that invest time in collectively creating shared agreements tend to experience more cohesiveness necessary for success in accomplishing thorny tasks (Valenzuela, 2022a). These challenging undertakings may include uniting the teaching staff, revamping curriculum, aligning instruction, or implementing a new reading or mathematics initiative.

Adopting shared agreements fosters a shared vision and mutual understanding among teaching team members, which can lead to improved collaboration, fruitful professional partnerships, and the energy to handle tasks as they arise (Simons & Simons-Zahno, n.d.). Furthermore, agreements providing a framework for structured discussions can assist teaching teams in navigating complex issues and conflicts more effectively (Sparks & Many, 2015).

Here are the areas where our work has seen teaching teams collectively have greater impact by establishing shared agreements (Valenzuela, 2022a):

- **Establishing and maintaining better norms for teaching team work:** Shared agreements define how the team wishes to collaborate, communicate, and make collective decisions.
- **Effectively utilizing the time and talents of team members:** By collectively agreeing on how to work best together, teams can optimize each member's unique strengths and abilities.

- **Respecting the thoughts and ideas of every team member:** Shared agreements can foster an environment where every voice is heard and respected.
- **Articulating clear organizational and department goals and responsibilities:** Agreements and norms can be put forward, helping to ensure that everyone is aligned with the overarching mission and objectives of the teaching team and educational institution.
- **Providing healthy parameters for difficult discussions and problem solving:** Shared agreements can help the team set the necessary guidelines for approaching and resolving challenging issues.

Before proceeding, it is critical for your teaching team members to embrace the shared agreements strategy and the listed benefits as a compass for fostering the collaboration required for achieving remarkable results within your unique school setting. Read, unpack, and discuss the benefits together—do not rush this process—and make sure everyone gets on the same page about how you will work together. The subsequent sections equip you with the essential guidance and strategies to solidify your developed shared agreements as the bedrock for your team's success.

Prioritizing Shared Agreements: *Building Highly Functional Teaching Teams*

Creating synergy within teaching teams is a complex challenge, with several moving parts necessitating the cultivation of communal relationships anchored by shared norms and expectations. Communal relationships, as defined in the field of psychology, refer to relationships in which individuals assume responsibility for the welfare of others they are in commune with ("Communal Relationships," n.d.). Scholarly insights underscore the pivotal role of establishing shared agreements for people working together cohesively (Hogan, 2022). Now, briefly consider our relationships beyond the workplace, like our partnerships or our children at home. At some point, we may find it beneficial to sit down with them to establish norms and agreements regarding our respective roles within the relationship. Setting clear expectations can also extend to planning a trip or organizing a family vacation.

Through our collective roles as coaches and thought partners in various schools, we have collaborated with numerous teaching team and school leaders actively seeking strategies to staff schools effectively, provide support during times of crisis, enhance instructional practices, and offer more constructive feedback to their teaching staff. Yet, amidst these priorities, one crucial aspect often remains overlooked—the development of shared norms and agreements between teaching team members and, more broadly, among the school's faculty and staff. Consider for a moment the increased potential for more contented and cooperative teaching team members.

Imagine the positive impact these leaders can have on staff morale and the retention of "happy" school employees when their voices are heard and actively included in shaping the environment in which they collaborate. It is now a place of their own creation—so buy-in is greater.

Navigating Challenges and Establishing Trust Through Shared Agreements

Before your teaching team ventures into creating its unique set of shared agreements, it is essential to recognize the multifaceted challenges that may accompany the ideation process. For example, two members of your teaching team have had a difficult relationship with one another, and trust has been broken so much that they are both weary and lukewarm about sharing their heartfelt agreements with one another. Leaders understanding the unique challenges impacting their team and successfully learning to navigate them is essential for achieving the desired synergy and collaborative spirit within the teaching team. For this purpose, in the subsequent paragraphs of this section, we will also delve into the critical role of trust building in the shared agreement creation process.

While division and personal conflicts among teaching team members are a severe detriment to teaching teams, they are not the only sources of discord preventing colleagues from collaborating effectively. Other happenings at the school such as negative student behavior or directives from the district central office may need addressing as well. Undoubtedly, in today's schools, district leaders, principals, and teaching teams have an arduous road when striving to mold staff and teaching faculty into highly functional, synergistic, student-focused teams, all in agreement on how best to work together for the benefit of one another and the students. The gravity of these challenges is highlighted by research findings that shed light on their prevalence in some American schools nationwide.

For instance, high levels of stress and burnout among some teaching staff members (Agyapong et al., 2023) may hinder the willingness of the teaching team to form shared agreements. Similarly, decreased job satisfaction and enthusiasm for remaining in the teaching profession (Toropova et al., 2021) can hinder the willingness of some teaching team members to engage in collaborative efforts. Moreover, high teacher turnover rates due to dissatisfaction with their job (Toropova et al., 2021) can disrupt the continuity of shared agreements, impacting the stability of the teaching team. Furthermore, the research shows a strong correlation between low teacher morale and lowered student learning outcomes (Kuhfeld, Soland, & Lewis, 2022; Lieberman, 2022), highlighting the urgency for teaching team leaders to address these challenges strategically.

Establishing *trust* is a foundational element that can be leveraged to navigate these multifaceted challenges effectively. Unfortunately, building trust is not simple; it must be consistently earned and established over time, especially for individuals who have experienced significant previous letdowns. To address establishing trust effectively within your teaching team, consider the following strategies:

1. **Encourage open communication:** Foster open and truthful communication to build trust among teaching team members. Encouraging everyone to speak from the heart and be open to feedback is vital, particularly when dealing with diverse viewpoints and differing philosophies. This allows everyone to feel heard (Valente et al., 2020).
2. **Address past conflicts:** Acknowledge the importance of addressing past conflicts and discord among the team members. Research supports the importance of resolving differences (Rinehart Kathawalla & Mehta, 2022; Valente et al., 2020).
3. **Engage in mediation and conflict resolution:** Recognize that in some cases, mediation and conflict resolution may be necessary to move forward. This aligns with research highlighting tensions and conflicts among educators (Valente et al., 2020) and hierarchical divisions (Rinehart Kathawalla & Mehta, 2022).

In short, implementing trust-building strategies to address the issues between others, head-on, enables teaching teams to lay the foundation for trust, collaboration, and positive vibes to exist. These strategies are relatively easy to apply but essential components of successful shared agreement creation and ultimately achieving synergy within teaching teams. The following vignette by Dr. Serbrenia Sims, superintendent of Surry County Public Schools, describes how two teachers on a middle school teaching team were able to resolve their long-standing differences by engaging in the development of shared agreements with colleagues applying the strategies of open communication and addressing past conflicts.

Cindy, a veteran educator with 15 years of teaching experience, was on a teaching team at a middle school. For years, she maintained a long-standing grievance with Mike, a colleague on the sixth-grade teaching team. Their differences in life philosophies and classroom approaches to student discipline led to several strained interactions, creating noticeable tension that adversely affected the culture in the teaching team. Despite their differences, Cindy and Mike shared a deep commitment to their students' learning and well-being. They did not initially say it, but they both recognized the urgency of addressing their conflicts so that they and the teaching team could collaborate effectively and not be a stumbling block in the path of the school's progress.

Cindy, Mike, and their other teaching team members decided to work together to develop shared agreements. They naturally adhered to open communication strategies during this process and addressed past conflicts. As they engaged in honest and heartfelt conversations, they understood each other's perspectives better. It was not easy, but their shared commitment to their students served as a unifying force, enabling them to find common ground and mutual respect over time. Their teaching team leader offered them mediation, but Cindy and Mike declined the opportunity as they could settle their differences independently. Ultimately, they cultivated the collegiality required for their teaching team to focus wholeheartedly on students, fostering a more harmonious and productive culture and environment in the school. ●

The aforementioned strategies can provide the needed foundation for nurturing trust, unity, and collaboration within your teaching team. When leaders encourage honest communication and, when necessary, address conflicts and grievances, the path can be created for a more cohesive and productive team. It won't be easy, but with committed team members, it's very much doable. Now, we will delve into practical steps to guide your teaching team through creating and sustaining your unique set of shared agreements and team norms.

Five Practical Steps for Creating and Sustaining Shared Agreements

The following steps are not the holy grail for capturing every teaching team's shared agreements—we have seen teams set their own process with successful results. Instead, these steps can provide process and structure within a flexible framework, allowing teams to adapt and customize as needed to meet the needs of their unique contexts.

Step 1: Cover the Basics (3–4 Minutes)

Select one facilitator who should begin by uplifting some basic agreements that correspond to all, if not most, of the teaching team members. Providing tangible examples of good agreements for teaching teams to have is a helpful scaffold for anyone who needs modeling for how to proceed. Examples of agreements the facilitator can introduce and unpack for the group may include some of the following:

- **Ensure everyone participates:** This doesn't mean everyone always has to speak, but participation requires active listening when another team member speaks.
- **Cultivate a safe space:** Create a teaching team where team members are comfortable speaking honestly while remaining open to feedback when their words do not land as intended or negatively impact others in the group.
- **Listen from the lens of empathy:** Encourage empathetic listening while acknowledging that we do not have to agree with the opinions of others—instead, we gain insight into their perspective.

- **Align intent with impact:** Team members strive to ensure that their intent matches the impact of their words.
- **Lead with self-awareness:** Know where you are currently and regroup as needed to bring your best self to the teaching team discussions and activities.

Step 2: Address Must-Haves and Deal-Breakers (5-7 Minutes)

Individually, each team member can reflect on their must-haves and deal-breakers in an ideal working environment. The facilitator should underscore the importance of self-reflection during this step. Teaching team members should invest time to think deeply about their values and how they can manifest within their working environment. It is vital for each team member to be clear about their must-haves and what qualifies as deal-breakers for them. These identified items should be classified as non-negotiables—elements one isn't willing to compromise on. Often people make concessions on their non-negotiables, resulting in unhappiness, resentment, and at times a toxic environment. Getting clear about our true values and wishes is the purpose of this step. We may find that gaining this level of clarity resonates in other areas of our lives too.

To streamline this process, direct every teaching team member to jot down their thoughts on a piece of paper folded down the middle. One side should list their must-haves and the other their deal-breakers. After they complete their initial drafts, have them revise their lists, only retaining their non-negotiable items. This approach is powerful for visualizing, thinking, and opening honest discussions in the subsequent steps of this process.

Facilitator's Note: You may find that the suggested 5–7-minute time frame for this activity doesn't suffice for your teaching team. Add more time as needed, emphasizing prioritizing thoughtful reflection.

Step 3: Discuss the Culture You're Building (8 Minutes)

This step is crucial as it allows team members to speak from the heart, explaining the observable behaviors and culture they would like to see happen because of creating the shared agreements. Take your time with this discussion; allow everyone the needed air space to express their thoughts and aspirations freely. Consider the following question prompts for getting conversations going:

- How do you visualize our interactions and relationships within this teaching team, resulting from the shared agreements we collectively create?
- What behaviors or actions can we commit to as a professional learning community to create a culture of trust, collaboration, and open dialogue daily?
- How will the culture and dynamic we create between us benefit our students and improve their learning environment and their learning outcomes?

Step 4: Get Everyone Involved (6 Minutes)

On large chart paper using markers, welcome everyone to add one or two agreements. You can use a tool like Nearpod or Google Docs to do this virtually instead. During this step, encourage the teaching team members to discuss or explain the agreements they added, if needed. This discussion can help ensure that all agreements are clearly understood and worded to reflect the group's intentions. Reiterate to everyone that the goal is to co-create shared agreements that every teammate can commit to and uphold. After all the agreements are captured, the facilitator should consolidate them for redundancy and make a manageable list.

Step 5: Share Your Teaching Team's Agreements (1 Minute)

Once refined, the list can be posted virtually or in spaces where the teaching team frequently meets. We recommend making it a regular but doable practice by having teams silently scan and reflect on the list at the start of every meeting. Regularly revisiting and reflecting on shared agreements and norms helps honor the time the team took to initially develop them and reinforces the team's commitment to upholding them. This brief practice invites anyone to discuss how the agreements are upheld as needed and allow for revisions. This step takes little time and provides space for conversation as needed.

In this vignette, the principal of Thomas Hunter Middle School in Mathews County, Virginia, Laurel Byrd, describes her teaching team's first experience with creating shared agreements.

My first experience with shared agreements was working with Jorge at the middle school where I was principal for 8 years. Since I knew my staff well, I loved seeing Jorge model the process and watch it break barriers for him and the staff to communicate and work together effectively. In August, I became the principal of a middle/high school in a different district. I didn't know the teachers, the culture, or the history well, so in my first meeting with the teacher leadership team, I used the process of creating shared agreements. At each meeting, I review them before we begin.

The impact of this has been amazing. Once the team realized that the agreement was going to be kept and honored, the atmosphere of trust was rapidly established. The feedback that I get from this group is honest and reasoned and creates forward movement. For me as the new principal, it allowed for identifying areas of strength and weakness. I also quickly found a group of teachers that I trust to give me an honest evaluation of situations that come up so that I can make an informed decision. The teachers' initial reaction was gratitude and relief. They relaxed and felt free to be honest in their concerns and continue to feel empowered to share their expertise. ●

Chapter Summary

Chapter 1 centers on the challenges teaching teams face in establishing and maintaining effective collaboration among the teaching staff to benefit students. We emphasize the importance of establishing shared agreements and norms as the foundation for teams discussing what improved collaboration in their space should look like. Creating shared agreements will take some time on the front end, and the process may be clunky—especially in spaces where open discussion is not the norm. We have personally witnessed improved collegial rapport in spaces where agreements are co-created and then honored by teaching teams. This is not a step we recommend your team skips.

The chapter also delves into the challenges teaching teams often must address to make their shared agreements successful, such as low educator morale and divisions between colleagues. The advice and strategies provide insights into understanding the intrinsic motivations of resistant colleagues, building trust, and addressing past conflicts, if needed, within the safe parameters of the teaching team.

Once a team establishes trust, building these shared norms together is a great next step in launching a truly productive and supportive workplace. Lastly, the chapter outlines practical steps for creating and sustaining your developed shared agreements and segues nicely into the following chapter, emphasizing the need for providing teachers with effective feedback.

Reflective Prompts for Teaching Team Members

1. Think of a time when you faced challenges collaborating with a colleague(s). What underlying issues hindered trust and open communication? How might having shared agreements established have helped improve that dynamic?
2. Reflect on the must-haves and deal-breakers you outlined. What may they look like within your teaching team? How can communicating these values enhance professional relationships with your colleagues?
3. Envision the school culture and climate you want to help create through your teaching team's shared agreements. What specific behaviors and actions do you know will contribute to a culture of trust and open communication with individuals where it previously did not exist?

Reflective Prompts for Teaching Teams

1. As a teaching team, discuss the challenges in working together effectively. How can co-creating to establish a set of shared agreements and norms help address those challenges to improve team collaboration?
2. Discuss everyone's must-haves and deal-breakers within the context of the teaching team's work. How can understanding one another's values lead to a happier and more productive teaching team?
3. Envision the school culture and climate your teaching team aims to establish and maintain through co-creating shared agreements. How can the teaching team's shared agreements positively impact student engagement, as well as academic achievement, and create an intellectually safe school environment?

CHAPTER 2

Empowering Teachers

Effective Strategies for Providing Feedback

This chapter builds on the foundation created by teaching teams establishing shared agreements in the previous chapter. We now delve into a critical aspect of unifying the path toward instructional innovation by establishing constructive approaches to providing teachers with feedback they can readily act upon. We emphasize the importance of effective communication to support teacher growth, self-efficacy, and overall teaching effectiveness. As teaching team leaders and educators, we understand that teaching conditions are not steadily variable. Instead, they are often dynamic—changing drastically in an instant—requiring continuous growth and adaptation, especially in expertly pivoting as job issues arise and need addressing.

Drawing from research insights and our personal experiences in leading schools and teaching teams, this chapter provides six practical guidelines that teaching team leaders, administrators, principals, and instructional coaches can use to deliver valuable feedback. We emphasize the need for customized and tailored approaches based on teachers' unique needs and performance levels. Additionally, we explore strategies for providing feedback to outstanding performers, motivating those who may need it, and supporting struggling teachers. Finally, the chapter concludes with a helpful feedback protocol to encourage productive discussions rather than one-way communication following classroom observations.

The Impact of Feedback on Teachers' Confidence

When I began teaching, I did not have the confidence I have today. Lacking confidence was for a myriad of reasons—let's just say it wasn't instilled in me in my youth, nor did I understand how confidence and self-assurance were developed over time by learning to do smaller tasks well and accumulating successful experiences gradually.

Being both a people and boss pleaser at the time didn't help my confidence levels either. Nevertheless, wanting to do a good job, I was always eager to receive

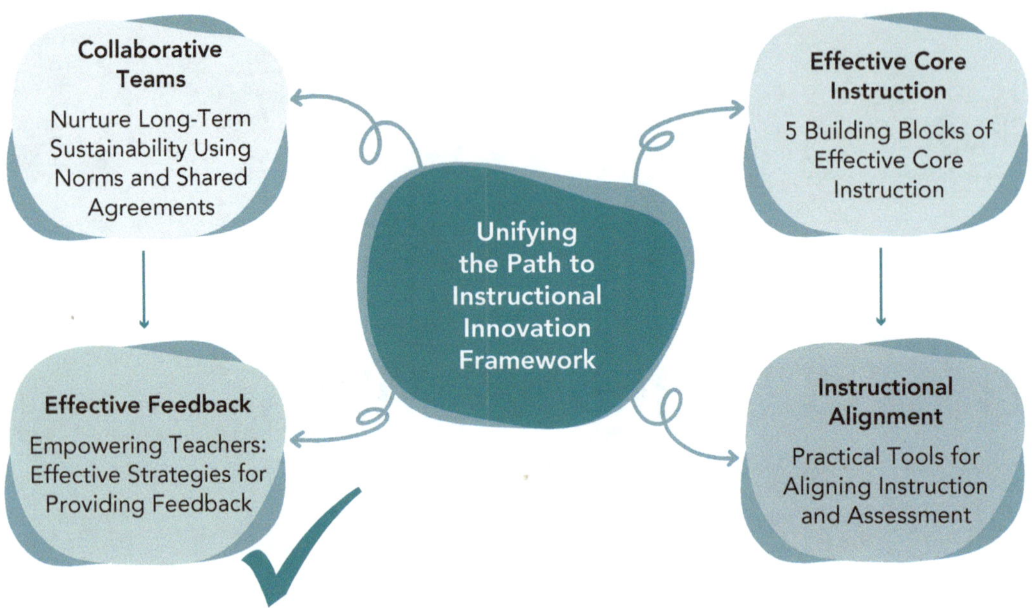

feedback and sought it from supervisors and colleagues I worked with closely. Unfortunately, some of the feedback I received then did not come from a good place or at all other than my annual evaluation. Other times, the feedback I received was just praise that affirmed something done well but did very little to help me improve my practice and teaching confidence.

Earlier in my teaching career, I couldn't put into words what I experienced like I can now. Not receiving the appropriate feedback was very frustrating and an emotionally crushing reality of my early teaching jobs. Back then I needed understandable and actionable feedback to grow in my teaching. As a result, my early teaching experience was plagued with uncertainty about my abilities and missed opportunities for students. I say this because I personally did not understand what high-yielding strategies were or have a research-informed playbook. No matter how well-intentioned educators are, we can't give students or others what we simply don't have.

Since then, my coaching work has shown me that many other teachers also struggle to get reliable feedback that addresses their most significant concerns from their building administrators. This is why this information is in Chapter 2 of this book written to empower teaching teams. Good teaching oftentimes begins with good leadership.

Fostering Confidence and Self-Efficacy Through Timely Feedback

We all know teachers help in shaping the future of American society. Unfortunately, our profession is not without its challenges—especially in current times with so many educators contemplating leaving their teaching jobs (American University

School of Education, 2022). Teaching team and school leaders, in general, need a healthy, confident, and vibrant teaching staff. We do not mean one without flaws—no one or nothing is ever perfect. A leader reading this might ask, "What can I do to uplift my teaching staff?" or "How can our teaching team help?"

Begin by clarifying the team's desired outcomes—timely feedback along with modeling the right teaching strategies to foster your teaching staff's overall confidence in their teaching abilities. Consider establishing rapport by employing timely feedback that is kind, frequent, helpful, and personalized to the receiver. We suggest you begin small by nurturing their self-efficacy—specifically, their belief in their ability to carry out essential tasks pertaining to core instruction. The building blocks of core instruction along with an adaptable teaching structure will be addressed in the following chapter on pages 45–53.

Before proceeding, let us make a distinction between confidence and self-efficacy. Self-confidence in this context is broader about overall teaching abilities. Self-efficacy is more task-specific—but they are interrelated. In his seminal work, Albert Bandura (1977) introduced *self-efficacy* to suggest that people's confidence in their abilities can significantly impact their internal motivation and decision making.

Additionally, people with higher self-efficacy may experience lower stress levels and cultivate positive outlooks for their challenges (Cherry, 2024). Reflecting on our personal and professional experiences, we have found this to be true. Furthermore, the more self-efficacy we developed for various tasks, the more our overall confidence in teaching and leadership grew.

Effective feedback can be the paramount tool for instructional leaders to use to enhance both mindsets and teaching. But it's important not to rush in—remember that feedback is variable (Valenzuela, 2022b) and should not be one-size-fits-all. New research even suggests that common ways of providing teachers with feedback may not always be effective (Burns, 2023). Therefore, we must learn how to always provide feedback well and in the relevant context of the teachers we support. Teaching team leaders should consider and incorporate the science of feedback in their leadership style, plans, words, and customization of information delivery to the teaching and school staff so they can maximize its impact.

As you and your team dive into this chapter, ponder how well your feedback is received by the teaching staff. Does it affirm where teachers are currently and convey where and how they need to level up? Feedback is more than an exchange of comments or a pat on the back—it is a powerful tool that can profoundly enhance self-efficacy for specific tasks and, consequently, boost the overall confidence of the teachers supported by your teaching team. This, in turn, strengthens their capacity to inspire and educate the youth within your schoolhouse effectively.

In the subsequent sections of this chapter, we will explore the intricate relationship between feedback, teacher self-efficacy, and overall confidence, uncovering how intentional and effective feedback can empower the educators you and your team support, along with a playbook for developing an authentic and purposeful feedback style.

Six Guidelines for Giving Meaningful Feedback

Remember, the feedback we provide must have the purpose of uplifting and empowering our teaching staff. Teaching team leaders can raise confidence in teachers by being more intentional about when and how to provide feedback by structuring conversations around what they observe in learning walks (Boss, 2018) or informal observations (Plotinsky, 2021). In this context, we strongly suggest that teaching teams keep feedback nonevaluative, constructive, and solely to improve instruction and build teacher confidence. Consider using these simple universal guidelines we gleaned from our practice (Valenzuela, 2022b):

1. **Feedback is variable and should not be one-size-fits-all.** Instead, tailor discussions to someone doing an excellent job, someone doing well but who could be better, or someone not working up to par. (See elaboration as follows.)
2. **Engage in dialogue, not monologue.** You build trust by sharing and using airtime to learn from teachers while constantly engaging them collegially, even during difficult conversations.
3. **Do not bombard teachers with unclear information.** That can convey weak leadership. It can confuse newbies and be off-putting to those who know better.
4. **Focus on the impact on student learning while respecting what teachers know about their students.** We find that teachers are the most prominent experts on the needs of their learners. So, listen to what they have to say even when examining measures of student achievement from assessments or student outcomes gleaned from surveys about their attitudes, confidence, and self-efficacy for learning.
5. **Make feedback quick when implementing a new initiative.** For example, if adopting a new strategy or approach does not work in specific spaces, this should become known to the teaching staff as soon as it is discovered. They will likely already know and resent being made to adhere needlessly.
6. **Critique work, not people.** By keeping the discussions to ways of improving teachers' abilities instead of things about them that they may not be able to change, teaching teams can get more buy-in.

Using these recommendations, here is how teaching team leaders and administrators can instill confidence in their teaching staff by differentiating and personalizing feedback.

Tailoring Feedback for Exemplary Performers

Teaching team and school leaders must acknowledge the value of exceptional teachers as invaluable assets to their schools. These educators foster student success and serve as role models for colleagues. Therefore, employ feedback strategies that show them loyalty and respect. Feedback to these teachers should be positive and convey appreciation (Medhi, 2024) for doing an excellent job and work well done. Get to know your exceptional folks to learn how they wish to receive good feedback—doing so can help nurture trust and commitment for the long haul. This will prove invaluable during a crisis or when the chips fall.

Excellent teachers know their value and will likely have a preference for how they like to receive feedback from others. A well-thought-out thank-you note may make some feel valued and confident. Others may want recognition in front of colleagues or more autonomy in teaching content they are passionate about. Excellent teachers have high value and should be treated as such. School leaders can leverage positive feedback opportunities to create an interchange of ideas to learn what works and what does not at the school or for particular students.

Feedback for Those Just Needing a Nudge

Providing feedback to teachers unaware of the areas they need to improve can be difficult for school leaders—especially if the person sees their performance as exemplary. In this case, they must trust that what we are telling them is for the refinement of their teaching. We need to build rapport and trust but also be honest with them. Here are some adaptable speaking points for a fictitious scenario to affirm them but still inform them of an area of need.

> *"It is clear that you are very passionate about teaching this unit, but I noticed that sometimes your passion does not allow room for students to ask clarifying questions during the direct instruction portion of your lesson. I saw that two kids raised their hands, but you did not call on them. Did you see their hands raised? Consider how this made them feel. How can student questions help clarify what they need to do during work time?"*

Remember, timely and truthful feedback aims to help grow teachers' confidence and teaching abilities—thus ultimately improving student learning outcomes. By addressing their areas of improvement cautiously and with empathy for those who just need a nudge, we can help them become more effective educators.

Supporting and Nurturing Struggling Teachers

We have all seen teachers struggling and needing more development for teaching know-how and classroom management. There is nothing wrong with being a beginner needing assistance, which could be for various reasons. As mentioned in the introduction to this book, some may be career switchers, be new to the job, or have only received textbooks and lectures without modeling in their preservice program. Regardless of their path to the education profession, these folks need to know that their teaching team is there to help them level up in a supportive and affirming environment.

Furthermore, struggling teachers need to feel their supervisors have their back, along with the belief that they have the potential to improve. Therefore, do not hold them accountable for what they do not know yet—instead, help them build confidence by setting clear pathways to success and keeping feedback kind, honest, and ongoing. Clear pathways to success can include norms and protocols outlining steps to completing deliverables, working well with others, contacting parents, and increasing capacity in their teaching abilities. Lastly, make sure your feedback doesn't put all the expectations and deliverables on teachers. Ask questions that reflect on better ways for you to support them. Here are some adaptable examples:

- "What can I do to best support you?"
- "Do you have the tools and resources you need to succeed?"
- "Are our timelines respectful of your time and workflow?"
- "Do you have any questions about our expectations?"

A Protocol for Providing Teachers Effective Feedback

Now that you have a sense of the feedback requirements the teachers you support may have, the ability of your teaching team to provide them with actionable and confidence-building feedback is crucial. Feedback must guide them toward growth, increased task self-efficacy, and teaching effectiveness. To empower your teaching team leaders, administrators, and instructional coaches with a structured approach to feedback using a straightforward and adaptable protocol, see Figure 2.1.

FIGURE 2.1: TEACHER FEEDBACK PROTOCOL

PROCESS	TIME	PERSON(S)
Clarification Following a separate classroom observation, the admin asks clarifying questions for supporting their feedback; the teaching staff makes clarifications.	2 Minutes	Admin and Teacher
Affirmations: "I Saw . . ." Admin begins the conversation by validating good teaching practice and sharing what they saw in alignment with performance expectations; the teaching staff listens.	3 Minutes	Admin
Sharing Concerns: "I Wonder . . ." Admin kindly shares concerns (e.g., teaching practice "lacks follow-through of the performance expectations" or "needs further development"); the teaching staff listens.	3 Minutes	Teacher
Providing Assistance: "Consider Using . . ." Admin shares ideas, strategies, and resources for improving teaching practice; the teaching staff listens and may respond.	3 Minutes	Teacher

PROCESS	TIME	PERSON(S)
Reflection and Open Conversation The teaching staff expresses what they heard from admin and steps they will take to make improvements; both admin and teaching staff may engage in open conversation.	5 Minutes	Admin and Teacher
Total	**16 Minutes**	

Adapted by Jorge Valenzuela of Lifelong Learning Defined, Inc.

Some leaders may naturally have the gift of providing feedback effortlessly, and others will need a scaffold like this protocol. We crafted this protocol to be a partner for instructional leaders looking to have impactful feedback conversations with their teachers. Use its structure to guide what you need to say affirmatively and constructively.

The protocol is powerful because of its foundation—it is research-informed (Bandura, 1977; Boss, 2018; Medhi, 2024; Plotinsky, 2021) and rooted in our own educational leadership experiences. It also aligns with the guidelines discussed in the earlier sections of this chapter. Whether you support exemplary performers, those needing a nudge, or struggling teachers, this protocol can be customized to meet their needs. As you prepare to have these conversations, remember to make feedback a tool for improvement, not evaluation.

Using the Protocol for Role-Play Practice

In our workshops, incorporating role play into practice using the protocol has proven effective for teaching teams. Here are two fictitious scenarios your team can use.

Scenario 1: Providing Feedback to a Struggling Teacher

Jessica is a middle school teacher struggling with her first teaching assignment. She loves teaching and is very passionate about working with students. This is evident in Jessica's welcoming and warm demeanor when interacting with students. Currently, she needs help understanding her teaching content and how to manage her students in group work. Teaching team leader X observed Jessica's class and must now give feedback to support her confidence and guide her in her teaching journey. Empathizing with the challenges of being a new teacher, teaching team leader X assures Jessica that gradual improvement takes time. Teaching team leader X affirms Jessica's passion for her students, emphasizes the significance of adopting high-yielding strategies for enhanced classroom outcomes, and is very specific about which strategy would work well for Jessica.

Scenario 2: Providing Feedback to a Teacher Who Needs a Nudge

Bob has taught at the same elementary school for the past five years and is considered by his colleagues as a seasoned teacher. He has an excellent rapport with his students but needs help identifying the right high-yield strategies to engage all his learners. After observing Bob's teaching, teaching team leader X provides constructive feedback to boost Bob's confidence and refine his teaching approach. Teaching team leader X begins by offering Bob affirming feedback on what he saw him do well and addresses his challenges with understanding which high-yielding strategies would work well in his class. Recognizing that Bob has not received appropriate training, teaching team leader X assures him that professional development will be held soon. Teaching team leader X emphasizes the significance of adopting high-yielding strategies for enhanced classroom outcomes and is very specific about which strategies would work well for Bob during the mini-lesson and group work portions of his daily teaching.

In this vignette, principal Laurel Byrd perfectly illustrates the use of the feedback protocol from her personal practice.

Giving feedback to teachers in a way that produces growth and change can be tricky at times, particularly when you are limited by an established "form." The "I saw . . . I wonder" protocol for feedback (see Figure 2.1) is a wonderful way to open a conversation and reflection on practice with teachers! The power of asking a good question cannot be understated. Whether it's a teacher asking students or administrators asking teachers, a great question will spark learning and contemplation. Very often, as teachers are answering your question, they will find their own answers.

I observed a teacher who was new to our district and only in the first few years of their career. Classroom management was definitely a struggle. As we sat down for the postobservation, the teacher was nervous and a bit teary eyed. "In my previous district we all just got criticized. No one ever helped me. I'm afraid that you are going to fire me!"

First, that's a terrible way to retain teachers! At this point, saying anything negative would not be helpful either! As an administrator, I try not to pass up an opportunity to support and coach. So, after reassuring this teacher, I used this protocol to open a conversation. When I asked, "What could you do differently when this happens in your room?" the teacher opened up. After describing the strategies she already used, she said, "You know, I've tried different things, but I am struggling with this. Can you help me?" Yes! We worked together to put strategies in place to help—and I'm happy to say that improvements were made! This level of trust and partnership would not have happened without time for questions and reflection. ●

Chapter Summary

In Chapter 2, we focus on empowering the teaching team and instructional leaders with insights and tools for providing effective feedback to their school's teaching staff. Leveraging the empathy cultivated through the development of shared agreements highlighted in the previous chapter, this chapter outlines the logical next steps teaching team leaders can take to provide timely and, most importantly, actionable feedback. The importance of teaching teams communicating effectively and modeling for teachers is further emphasized in this chapter. Doing so will help foster their self-efficacy for specific tasks and overall confidence in their teaching abilities. Teachers should not feel that they're going at it alone in their teaching assignments—especially the ones new to our profession or ones facing challenges finding their footing.

Furthermore, the content in this chapter draws from research insights and my personal experiences of successfully leading schools and teaching team instructional innovation efforts. Six practical guidelines for delivering valuable feedback are discussed—calling for instructional leaders to tailor feedback based on the unique needs and performance levels of the teachers they serve. We explore various feedback strategies catering to exemplary performers, those needing a nudge, and those currently struggling.

We conclude by introducing a structured feedback protocol that teaching team leaders can use as a guide for having productive discussions following classroom observations. Readers should glean from this chapter that feedback is a tool for helping teachers improve and refine practice rather than evaluation. The know-how teaching team leaders require for effectively addressing their teaching staff will serve them well as we transition to the next chapter and learn about the five building blocks of effective core instruction, along with our recommendations for carrying out daily instruction.

Reflective Prompts for Individual Teaching Team Members

1. Think of a time when your confidence needed boosting in an earlier teaching assignment. What factors challenged you most to feel confident in your teaching ability? How might receiving effective feedback from your direct supervisor or trusted colleagues have assisted you then?
2. Reflect on the teachers your teaching team currently serves. What can you do specifically to help them become more confident in their teaching? Given their needs and levels, how can you tailor your feedback approach for individual teachers?
3. Envision your entire school beaming with confident and effective teachers. Consider the impact these teachers would have on their students. What specific attributes and skills would these teachers possess? What can you do right now to make positive strides toward helping your teaching team make this a reality?

Reflective Prompts for Teaching Teams

1. As a teaching team, discuss confidence and self-efficacy in the context of teaching. How can the teaching team provide feedback that helps teachers make gradual improvements in how they view their teaching abilities? What are the factors of effective feedback?
2. Discuss the role of feedback in the school's teaching team's work. What steps will the teaching team take to ensure that feedback will be viewed as a tool for refinement rather than an evaluative tool? How will the teaching team earn the trust of the teaching staff in this regard, and how will success be measured?
3. Envision how the teaching team wishes to have teachers embrace the feedback they provide them. What are concrete ways to ensure feedback to every teacher is timely and actionable? What will teaching team leaders do if they are unsure of how to model specific strategies they recommend to teachers?

CHAPTER 3

The Five Key Building Blocks of Effective Core Instruction

This chapter builds upon the groundwork laid in the previous chapters, emphasizing team and relationship building for teaching team leaders. Now that we understand how effective collaboration can unfold, we introduce and elaborate on five crucial elements underpinning effective core instruction across diverse educational settings (Valenzuela, 2022c). The information in this chapter is meant to be informative about what constitutes good core instruction. Many of the strategies mentioned in this chapter will be elaborated on in greater detail in subsequent chapters.

Our objective is to help you grow your teachers by providing a solid foundation for confident teaching and instructional innovation without too much information overload. Adherence to these five elements not only enhances current teaching practices but also positions teachers to expand their teaching repertoire in the future. To aid your teaching team with unpacking and understanding this content, at the close of this chapter, we offer a practical strategy you can use to help engage, discuss, and internalize these foundational elements effectively.

First, we delve into recommendations for crafting a personalized curriculum closely aligned with state and local standards, student goals, interests, and specific learner profiles within the local or regional context. Second, we explore the intentional integration of literacy and numeracy skills throughout the curriculum to fortify students' foundational cognition and problem-solving abilities. Drawing on the insights of experts Robert Marzano and John Hattie, our third element defines and recommends versatile, high-yielding teaching strategies that serve multiple purposes, encompassing areas such as reading, writing, collaboration, and engagement.

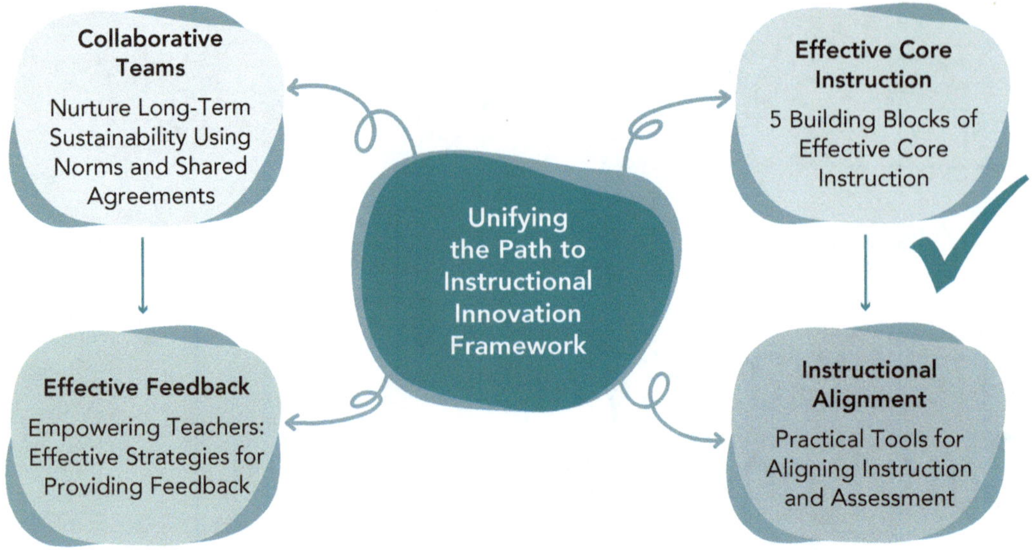

The fourth element provides practical methods for monitoring student engagement and academic achievement, offering assessments and gauges to determine learners' current standing and delivering timely feedback to facilitate their continuous growth. Last, we underscore the significance of self-reflection and soliciting feedback from colleagues and students as integral components for refining our impact as educators.

Mastery of these five elements empowers individual teachers and teaching teams to elevate their core instruction, establishing a robust, research-informed foundation for adeptly supporting all learners. Furthermore, the insights presented in this chapter extend beyond the classroom, offering valuable guidance for school and district leaders seeking to develop systemic or schoolwide instructional models.

Defining Core Instruction

A strong core or solid base is critical for any endeavor requiring building time and sustained effort. The popular expression "Rome was not built in one day" can be clearly understood by adding "but they laid brick every day." Real-world examples of where establishing a solid core makes building the rest possible may include fitness routines, long-term partnerships, and house constructions. The key here is for teaching team leaders to help teachers develop a strong foundation for teaching day-to-day. In Chapter 4 (page 57), we will provide instructional alignment and a simple structure for daily teaching. First, let's understand the components of good core instruction.

As an instructional coach, I often work with school and district leaders who initially contact me to focus on high-lift initiatives pertaining to some aspect of instructional innovation (multitiered system of support [MTSS], project-based learning [PBL], etc.). When necessary, we begin by helping them shore up their staff's ability to deliver effective core instruction (M. Bowen, 2021). This foundational tier is also known as Tier 1 instruction. Core instruction is the critical whole-group lessons teachers produce in primary subject areas that serve as a good backdrop for the differentiation strategies required to support struggling learners and students with diverse needs. Helping school leaders and teachers build competency for their core instruction over the years is the necessary groundwork for a dynamic and responsive educational environment.

For example, a school looking to begin or enhance implementing tiered instruction as part of an MTSS framework (Reading Horizons, 2024) may need guidance in identifying and carrying out the components of Tier 1 instruction (Metcalf, 2015) for establishing whole-group messages during their lessons. Tiers are crafted to challenge students at their appropriate ability levels. Similarly, schools looking to use a response-to-intervention (RTI) (Shapiro, n.d.) or PBL teaching model (Valenzuela, 2022d) may need similar guidance on a good starting point for planning and facilitating lessons in tandem with helping teachers determine their students' learning needs. Schools must recognize that, no matter how they teach or support interventions, understanding and implementing Tier 1 instruction is essential for building a strong foundation to support diverse learning needs.

To fortify the impact of these foundational principles, teaching teams should also recognize that it is not enough for teachers only to have a sound system for planning and facilitating relevant lessons. Teachers also need to monitor student engagement and learning intentionally. This deliberate approach allows for ongoing tweaking and refining practice from an informed approach. To support you and your teaching team in unifying the path to instructional innovation, we created a versatile framework to serve as a good starting point for outlining the essential elements of good core instruction. Each of the five blocks is designed to unify with the others to empower educators to implement core instruction effectively with lots of flexibility, fostering a mindset of foundational knowledge and continuous improvement within learning environments.

Five Must-Haves for Good Core Instruction

1. Designing Relevant and Personalized Curriculum

Curriculum refers to an evidence-based sequence of planned experiences aligned with standards and competencies, helping learners capture content concepts and applied skills (The Wing Institute, 2024). A robust and well-thought-out curriculum can follow local standards, graduate profiles, career skills, emotional intelligence skills, and students' unique interests. A curriculum personalized for specific learners is a powerful addition to any classroom. It serves as a road map for students' educational journeys, providing teachers with the guidance to lead them toward a comprehensive understanding of subjects and developing crucial skills necessary for success in academics and life.

Curriculum can be purchased, and many schools opt for this approach, especially for teachers new to the profession. While using purchased curriculum and scripted resources for core instruction is acceptable, we do not advise following them verbatim. As mentioned in the previous paragraph, personalizing the curriculum for your unique learners is crucial and ties to their buy-in. Failure to do so risks losing student engagement (Valenzuela, 2022e) due to a perceived lack of relevance. Teaching teams taking time to infuse their curriculum with elements that resonate with students' interests and experiences can enhance their engagement and create a more meaningful and effective learning experience (Valenzuela, 2022e).

To assist planning teams in designing core instruction (Valenzuela, 2022f) in meaningful and compelling ways for students, try the empathy mapping process (Valenzuela, 2021) along with a straightforward instructional alignment tool (Valenzuela, 2022g). For detailed guidance on adapting these tools effectively in curriculum mapping and development, refer to Chapter 4 (page 62). Empathy mapping can help you determine relevance for students, while the alignment tool offers a straightforward approach to mapping and aligning learning goals with assessments, lessons, and high-yielding instructional strategies—each a crucial component of sound core instruction.

2. Integrating Literacy and Numeracy Across Subject Areas

Undoubtedly, literacy and numeracy skills are the bedrock of academic and life success. Learners developing these skills in meaningful ways become prepared for reading, writing, reasoning, and problem solving across multiple disciplines. Text and mathematics permeate many aspects of students' lives (Victoria State Government Department of Education, 2024), and teaching teams must help teachers make sense of how to promote literacy and numeracy in their classes. We believe all teachers should intentionally support their students in developing these abilities. Even if you are not an English language arts (ELA) or mathematics teacher or are not utilizing a formal program for tiering and differentiation (e.g., MTSS, RTI), enhancing your core instruction should involve integrating literacy and mathematics to complement your lessons meaningfully.

Importance of the Science of Reading

Before providing our advice on how to embed literacy into teaching and learning for non-ELA teachers, we'd like to point out the importance of the science of reading in improving literacy skills. Educators who understand the cognitive processes activated in reading can make better-informed instructional decisions supporting reading development (National Center on Improving Literacy, 2022). According to the National Reading Panel Report (2000), learners must develop these five essential components of the science of reading:

1. **Phonological awareness:** Recognizing words as composed of smaller sounds
2. **Phonics:** Understanding that letters make sounds to form words
3. **Fluency:** Reading accurately and smoothly
4. **Vocabulary:** Building a rich understanding of words
5. **Reading comprehension:** Deriving meaning from text

Unfortunately, the data regarding the implementation of the science of reading aren't optimistic. *Education Week* reports the following (Heubeck, 2024):

- Licensure exams for teachers often overlook the five science-based components of reading proficiency.
- Only 25 percent of new teachers feel adequately prepared to teach reading using research-informed strategies.

Unfortunately, trying new instructional practices without connecting the relevant literature with practice for teachers is quite common in many schools. We encourage teaching teams to prioritize the foundational items (like the science of reading and the elements of core instruction), understanding that learning to do something new well takes time.

Promotion of Literacy Across Subject Areas

ELA integration isn't as difficult as non-ELA teachers may think. For instance, science, social science, and elective teachers can emphasize the reading and writing skills relevant to their content through daily reflective prompts such as exit tickets and visible thinking routines, requiring students to write and explain their thinking (Project Zero, n.d.). In Appendix A (page 151), resources are available for implementing Project Zero thinking routines to enhance critical thinking skills through reading and writing across various disciplines (Valenzuela, 2022h). Similarly, science, technology, engineering, and mathematics (STEM) teachers and computer science teachers can guide students in outlining the steps of the design process while emphasizing grammar, sentence structure, and proper citations. This approach significantly enhances students' literacy skills over time.

Additionally, encouraging students to create and rehearse presentation scripts can be a potent literacy-building activity that reinforces both speaking and listening skills. Without extensive planning, teachers can seamlessly incorporate these literacy-building activities into unit plans, projects, and daily teaching.

Promotion of Numeracy Skills Across Subject Areas

To build on activating literacy across subject areas, incorporating mathematics into unit plans is not as challenging as some people may think. Nonmathematics teachers can play a crucial role in helping learners enhance their basic knowledge of numbers by embedding numeracy skills into daily lessons and unit plans. Computation in activities such as performance tasks and product development allow students to develop real-world mathematics skills. Foundational knowledge can be constructed by building competence in the following areas:

- **Budgeting:**
  - Example: Students can learn to create a budget for themselves or others or analyze the budget of the county or city they live in (Study.com, n.d.).
- **Calculations:**
  - Example: Students can perform calculations related to experiments, daily spending, the economy, calculating growth and declining rates, concentrations, and converting units (Cuemath, n.d.).
- **Representing and interpreting data:**
  - Example: Students can collect data on preferences related to their learning content, create visual representations such as graphs and charts, and analyze and interpret the data to inform their decision-making and persuasion skills (Blankman, 2023).
- **Measurement and data analysis:**
  - Example: Students can learn to measure and analyze dimensions to design a 3D-printed object or create digital models using computers (Fluency & Fitness+, n.d.).
- **Relationships between numbers:**
  - Example: Students can explore the relationship between numerical data and various literary forms, such as analyzing the numerical symbolism in a specific piece of literature or studying the historical context using statistical trends (Peanut Butter Fish Lessons, n.d.).

These examples illustrate how various mathematics skills can be integrated across subject areas. In Appendix A (page 152), there is a curated list of websites to assist teachers in incorporating these mathematics skills. Additionally, we provide a comprehensive lesson and project planner balanced with fields designed to help teachers plan literacy and numeracy connections aligned with their curriculum and content area (see Appendix A, page 153).

3. Implementing High-Yielding Strategies for Effective Instruction

In the context of this book, high-yielding strategies refer to teaching and instructional approaches that have consistently produced significant and positive learning outcomes for learners (Learning Focused, n.d.). These strategies are evidence based and effective and, when adapted appropriately, often result in positive classroom engagement, academic growth, understanding, skill development, and retention of information across various subjects and grade levels (Hattie, 2009, 2023). These approaches are considered best practices in education and should be part of every teacher's playbook.

Consider a very talented football or basketball player who does not have the playbook while their teammates do. Even with great ability and talent, that player will struggle immensely and will not be able to compete at their best. For teachers, there is power in having a set of pedagogical strategies to lean on when seeking specific outcomes. High-yielding strategies and instructional scaffolds are what teachers should reach for when teaching a particular lesson. Having a set of go-to strategies for boosting critical thinking (Valenzuela, 2022h), cooperative learning (Merrill, 2019), and providing students effective and timely feedback (Valenzuela, 2022i) (among other items) can strengthen core instruction and Tier 2 and 3 interventions.

In our experience coaching teachers, many recognize the value of incorporating high-yielding strategies as a concept but often struggle with selecting specific strategies. Robert Marzano's research simplifies this process by outlining nine strategies (Technology & Learning, n.d.) proven to enhance student achievement across grade levels and content areas (see Table 3.1). Additionally, John Hattie's Visible Learning research (Corwin, 2024) serves as a trusted resource for helping educators understand and consider research to select strategies they can tailor to the specific context and goal they're looking to achieve.

TABLE 3.1: MARZANO'S HIGH-YIELDING INSTRUCTIONAL STRATEGIES (MARZANO ET AL., 2001)

INSTRUCTIONAL STRATEGY	PURPOSE
Identifying Similarities and Differences	Help students understand and use compare–contrast techniques.
Summarizing and Note-Taking	Teach students effective summarization and note-taking techniques.
Reinforcing Effort and Providing Recognition	Acknowledge students' hard work and achievements.
Homework and Practice	Assign purposeful homework and provide opportunities for practice.
Linguistic and Nonlinguistic Representations	Encourage the use of visual and kinesthetic representations of knowledge.
Cooperative Learning	Organize students into small groups to work together.
Setting Objectives and Providing Feedback	Communicate clear learning goals and provide constructive feedback.
Generating and Testing Hypotheses	Engage students in critical thinking and problem-solving activities.
Cues, Questions, and Advance Organizers	Use effective questioning techniques and provide clear organizers to introduce new content.

In Chapter 4 (page 60), we provide Table 4.1 for helping teachers align their instruction by selecting and organizing the high-yielding strategies they want to implement when delivering lessons. We highly recommend that teaching teams encourage teachers to try various strategies to gain insight into how they help learners succeed as they steadily improve their core instruction. They should learn the appropriate times to use the strategies because every strategy should not be used daily or in every lesson and project. To remove your guesswork, in this book, we have purposefully selected and adapted strategies that can produce high-yielding results.

4. Monitoring Student Engagement and Academic Achievement

In his meta-study of what works in education, researcher John Hattie (2009) asserts, "No manner of school reform will be successful until we first face and resolve the engagement problem" (p. 32). Academic research consistently establishes a robust correlation between student engagement and achievement, emphasizing its significance for teachers across grade levels and disciplines as an integral aspect of core instruction (Dyer, 2015). Teachers must assess all aspects: understanding how students feel about learning, identifying how they learn best, and gauging their grasp of the content. When this is done consistently, learning becomes a partnership between teachers and learners. Additionally, monitoring engagement and achievement provides teachers clarity about what's working and not working in regard to their core teaching for particular students.

Effectively monitoring student engagement goes beyond observing positive body language, eye contact, and active class participation; it requires intentional efforts. Poll Everywhere (2020) recommends specific strategies for meaningful engagement:

- Asking questions and leading discussions
- Observing participation in collaborative work by seeing how students respond in smaller settings
- Polling students using engagement surveys

To help you get started, here are some questions we thoughtfully crafted, adapted from SurveyMonkey (n.d.):

- Which classroom activities engage you the most?
- What's the best way to engage you in lessons?
- What are three ways that can improve your engagement levels?
- As your teacher, what can I do to better engage you?

Academic achievement should be monitored daily using formative assessments (Edutopia, n.d.). Informal formative assessments don't produce grades but are critical for informing teachers about how students are grasping the material. Good ones for strengthening core instruction may include thumbs-up responses (Edutopia, 2019), exit tickets (Edutopia, 2015), and quizzes. Formal formative assessments typically produce grades and are indicative of what students have mastered and where they need assistance within a particular subject area. Biweekly, end-of-unit, and benchmark assessments are metrics your district may have in place for you to use. In Chapter 4 (page 60), we provide Table 4.1 for helping teachers specify their various formative assessments for lessons.

While these types of assessments are common, they are not universal to all school systems across America. Many schools and districts have different policies or approaches for assessment practices and vary depending on their local education policies. We will, therefore, not cover a specific way to assess students academically beyond the examples of formative assessment mentioned in this paragraph.

5. Reflecting On and Improving Teaching Impact

Individual teachers can significantly improve their teaching impact by consistently receiving and reflecting on feedback from their students. This practice aids in refining their implementation of teaching strategies by better aligning with students' learning needs for their success. Hattie (2012) refers to this process as "knowing thy impact," emphasizing the significance of actively listening to students to gauge how our practice influences their engagement and learning outcomes. When teachers openly acknowledge potential blind spots in their teaching that might lead to misunderstandings, it can foster trust among students, encouraging honest communication about their learning experiences.

Teachers do not only have to seek feedback from students to improve their teaching impact; they can also seek to do so from trusted colleagues (Valenzuela, 2022b). Teachers receiving input and critique from each other for improving their practice is listed as a vital component of effective professional development (PD) in a review by Darling-Hammond et al. (2017). The review is robust and examined 35 methodologically rigorous studies demonstrating a positive link between teacher PD teaching approaches and learner outcomes (Darling-Hammond et al., 2017). One PD opportunity that we use within our teaching teams is learning walks. Learning walks can be conducted as an informal, structured observation between teachers, an excellent way to observe and be observed within a low-stakes setting (Valenzuela, 2022j). In Chapter 6 (page 87), we will provide guidelines for conducting and participating in learning walks between colleagues.

When receiving timely feedback is not commonplace or part of the culture within a teaching team, it can seem daunting for teachers looking to find their footing. Fostering a lifelong learner mindset can help ease anxiety associated with showing vulnerability. Lifelong learners actively pursue formal and informal education, training, and development for both career and personal advancement (Sanderson, 2023). When teachers consider themselves learners, it can be easier to have conversations with students and colleagues about the areas of our core instruction that we can improve. Excellent practice can focus on what is not working with our core teaching and particular students. Seeking the right strategies for improving our impact becomes intentional (see building block 4) instead of jumping on the latest teaching trend (see building block 3).

Surveying, polling, learning walks, and student conferences can improve teaching impact. Feedback questions don't have to be long or intellectually challenging, but they should be specific. I recommend keeping it simple and straightforward. Teachers can ask questions from either colleagues or students, such as the examples listed in Table 3.2. Of course, these are not set in stone but can be a helpful start for beginning constructive conversations.

TABLE 3.2: FEEDBACK QUESTIONS FOR ENHANCING TEACHING IMPACT

FEEDBACK QUESTIONS FOR COLLEAGUES	FEEDBACK QUESTIONS FOR STUDENTS
What aspects of my lesson did you find most effective, and why?	Which classroom activities help you learn the most?
Are there any areas where I could enhance student engagement or understanding in my facilitation?	What changes do you recommend I make to support your learning better?
Did you notice any strategies I used that could be improved?	What motivates you the most to engage and learn?
What suggestions do you have for refining the delivery or pacing of my lesson?	How can I improve as your teacher to enhance your learning experience?
How can I further support my students' learning beyond the classroom?	Do you feel seen and heard in my class? If not, what can I do better?

Important Note for Teaching Teams: These feedback questions are not meant to be universally applicable to every teacher or teaching scenario. They can be adapted to fit the context and can provide teachers looking to improve and refine their teaching impact with a starting point.

Unpacking Core Concepts: *Leveraging the Jigsaw Protocol*

As mentioned in the introduction to this chapter, the information presented is primarily meant to be informational—highlighting the five core concepts every teacher should know regarding their core instruction. However, your teaching team can unpack this information using the jigsaw protocol. The jigsaw protocol is a popular education strategy and excellent for chunking and unpacking informational text in participant-led expert teams during PD (Aronson et al., 1978) (see Figure 3.1).

FIGURE 3.1: JIGSAW PROTOCOL

PROCESS	TIME	PERSON(S)
Jigsaw Text and Form Expert Teams Chunk a selected text into manageable and smaller parts and form homogeneous expert participant groups. Assign a portion of the selected text to each expert team.	2 Minutes	Facilitator and Participants
Read, Analyze, and Explain Participant expert teams read and analyze text (annotating, highlighting, etc.) and explain their learning with each other.	10 Minutes	Participants
Synthesize Expert teams create a synthesis in the form of an artifact with three bullets: (1) Concept(s) defined, (2) Examples from the reading, and (3) Explanation of their main takeaways. Students who struggle with writing can create graphics or images.	6 Minutes	Participants
Teach Others Have all expert teams return to the heterogeneous group (e.g., the entire class) to present and discuss their learning.	2 Minutes	Facilitator and Participants
Complete the Jigsaw Participants reconvene in their homogeneous expert groups to align the learning from the other jigsaw pieces of text they learned from the other expert teams.	5 Minutes	Participants
Total	**25 Minutes**	

Adapted from Aronson (n.d.)

In this instance, the jigsaw activity can be leveraged to create an informal opportunity for your teaching team to explain targeted topics to each other while improving their overall understanding. Have the team break up into five groups to become "experts" in one of the five building blocks of core instruction, then share what they know in jigsawed groups with others who learned about different parts of the framework. Structure this by asking them to offer their own definitions and provide evidence from the reading and their practice while explaining it all casually. Adapt the steps in Figure 3.1 to clarify these steps and procedures.

Importance of Core Instruction

The following vignette describes how contributor Sara Leone and her colleagues at Summit Public Schools in Chicago, Illinois, improved teaching and learning by focusing on firming up core instruction.

Core instruction forms the foundation of our students' learning journey and plays a crucial role in their academic success. Postpandemic, as a district, we began looking at core instruction differently. We understood that in order to mitigate learning loss, our core instruction needed attention. By prioritizing our core instruction, it ensured a cohesive and consistent learning experience for all of our students, guaranteeing that they had a strong understanding of fundamental concepts prior to moving on to more complex topics.

As a district, previously, we had good intentions, but we were lacking in frameworks for instructional alignment to ensure that students received a consistent education across buildings and grade levels. Collectively, we identified what our district non-negotiables would be related to instruction, which gave us direction. Students would be presented with clear learning targets and participate in various activities throughout a lesson. Formative assessment would be embedded, and teachers would differentiate to meet the varying needs of all students. We felt that with well-structured core instruction, teachers could focus on implementing innovative teaching strategies and differentiation techniques to meet the diverse needs of their students. For us, core instruction is not a thing in education, but rather the *thing. Frankly, the best academic interventions are for naught if our core instruction is not solid. Once we accepted that we would never be able to intervene ourselves out of a core instructional problem, our efforts shifted to paying close attention to core instruction.* ●

Chapter Summary

This chapter explains five essential elements as building blocks for effective core instruction in diverse educational settings. Teaching team leaders can adapt these building blocks to provide teachers with a comprehensive understanding of what comprises good core instruction, creating a solid foundation they can build on throughout their teaching journeys. In subsequent chapters, we will offer a more in-depth explanation of the strategies mentioned in Chapter 3, but for now we just want you to gain a solid footing for core instruction. Moreover, this chapter lays the groundwork for confident teaching and instructional innovation by emphasizing personalized curriculum design, integrating literacy and numeracy across lessons, employing high-yielding instructional strategies in daily teaching, monitoring student engagement and achievement, and promoting self-reflection and feedback to monitor one's impact.

Building competency in these foundational elements over time can empower educators to elevate their core instruction, benefiting current practices and fostering a culture of continuous improvement. Furthermore, these insights can extend beyond the classroom, guiding systemic instructional models at the school and district levels.

The chapter culminates in a practical strategy using the jigsaw protocol, fostering deeper comprehension and discussion among teaching teams about these elements. Moving into Chapter 4, teaching teams should use these insights to align their written curriculum and facilitated instruction.

Reflective Prompts for Individual Teaching Team Members

1. Consider your previous understanding of good core instruction. Which concepts affirmed or challenged you most as you dove into the five building blocks of core instruction explained in this chapter? How might you begin implementing these concepts and practices to improve your own core instruction?
2. Reflect on the teachers your teaching team currently serves. What can you do to help them boost their understanding of solid core instruction? Given where they are currently regarding their understanding, how can you tailor your explanation for individual teachers?
3. Envision your entire school being on the same page about core instruction and using it as a foundation for consistently improving their pedagogy. Consider the impact these teachers would have on all students. What can you do right now to make positive strides toward helping your teaching team make this a reality?

Reflective Prompts for Teaching Teams

1. As a teaching team, discuss core instruction and the elements that can comprise its solid foundational building blocks. How can the teaching team begin helping the teachers they serve to develop their understanding and practices around these elements?
2. Discuss the current role of core instruction in your teaching team's school. What steps will the teaching team take to ensure that solid core instruction is the foundation of the school's instructional model? How will the teaching team include the teaching staff in the initial stages of this vital conversation?
3. Visualize how the teaching team wishes teachers to embrace the foundational five elements of good core instruction. What are the things that must be in place to facilitate this understanding amongst the teaching staff, and how will it benefit students? What will teaching team leaders do if they need help with how to proceed with helping teachers achieve the desired levels of understanding?

CHAPTER 4

Tools for Aligning Instruction and Assessment

This chapter expands on the previous chapter's discussion of the five foundational blocks of core instruction by ensuring teaching teams understand alignment in planning and executing daily lessons. The following are necessary steps teaching teams must take toward achieving instructional innovation as outlined in Part II of this book. The coherence between various teaching elements, including student learning goals, instructional strategies, assessments, and facilitation, is essential for effective teaching. Creating intentional alignment clarifies what is being taught, how it is being taught, and how learning is assessed, which align harmoniously to achieve the desired educational goals for students.

Within this chapter, we explore valuable tools teachers can use to align their instruction with their learning and assessment goals. We begin by discussing the importance of daily lessons having flow and alignment, emphasizing the need for a reservoir of trusted pedagogical strategies at our teaching disposal. The chapter then introduces an instructional alignment tool inspired by backward design methodology (Valenzuela, 2022g). It helps teachers map their instruction in alignment with formal and informal formative assessments and daily learning goals. We then provide a structure inspired by Samantha Bennett's (2007) teaching model that teachers can use during their teaching block to maximize differentiation strategies (Valenzuela, 2023).

Throughout this chapter, we offer practical examples and resources to illustrate how the tool and alignment strategies can be implemented to fidelity. Additionally, we include a video link for step-by-step guide to completing the tool quickly using new artificial intelligence apps. Moreover, the tools highlighted in this chapter can be used by teachers in any subject and content area, leading to more coherent and purposeful lessons for all students.

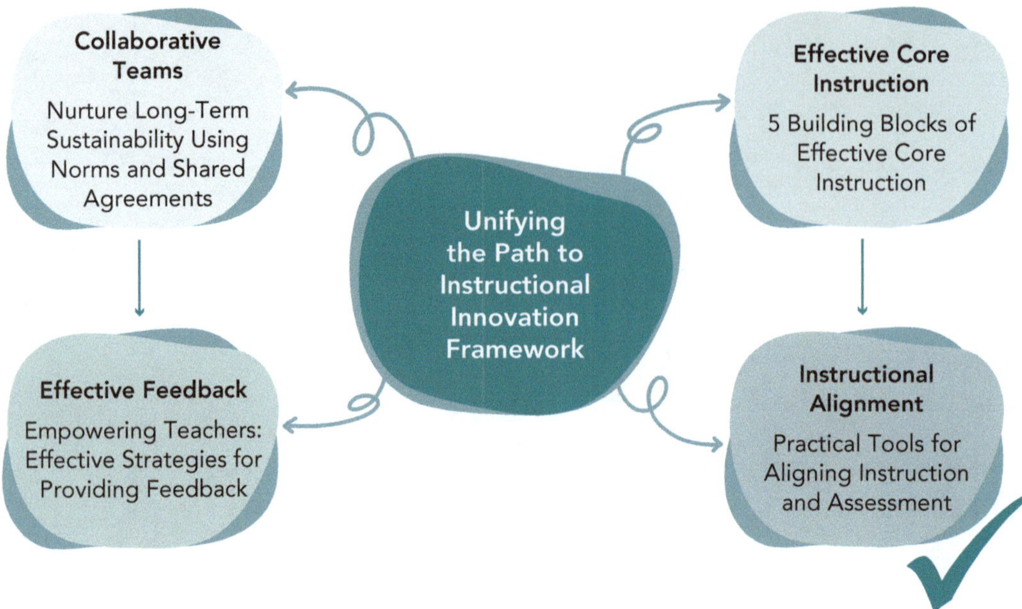

The Analogous Art of Instructional Alignment: Lessons From Fitness Applied to Teaching

Teaching at our best is like anything else we pursue—it is part science and part art. Sound teaching is an amalgam of learned and applied skills requiring time and patience, which we believe can be achieved quicker when there is intentional flow and alignment around core instruction. Achieving flow and alignment within daily lessons is akin to structuring a well-designed health and fitness routine. Success isn't an accident—continuous learning, planning, preparation, and execution need to happen first. Anyone achieving success in their fitness goals understands the meticulous planning and execution required of good regimens.

For example, people looking to achieve optimal health typically need to consider various factors to ensure their health and fitness goals are met, such as diet, strengthening their core (pelvis, stomach, hips, and lower back muscles), and performing physical exercises correctly. There is never a quick solution that doesn't require consistent attention to alignment and harmony between goals, planning, and execution. Otherwise, people may be winging their health and fitness ambitions because there isn't flow and alignment between their goals and what they must do to accomplish them. In the context of fitness, this is simple to understand. Now, let us apply a similar logic to aligning daily lessons.

The Importance of Flow and Alignment in Daily Lessons

Flow and alignment in teaching encompass more than just planning aligned lessons—they involve building on our core instruction and the art of facilitation. Instructional alignment within the context of this book goes beyond the lesson's outline and delves into how educators facilitate the learning process. It requires us to develop a daily plan for engaging students and to be open and prepared when we must pivot from that plan because our students require something different. It also requires understanding how assessment drives instruction (Miller, 2021) and the alignment between summative assessment, learning goals, formative assessment, high-yielding strategies, and scaffolds.

Classroom teachers need to have fluidity and a reservoir of trusted pedagogical strategies they know when to use to plan and facilitate instruction. These strategies must be part of methods for attacking daily instructional problems with flexibility to address unforeseen occurrences. Although there are many ways to teach, daily lessons must have flow and alignment. Several benefits are highlighted in research for both teachers and students when instruction is aligned:

Benefits for Teachers:

- **Clarity in Objectives:** Teachers can align lessons more effectively for students when understanding the intended learning outcomes within their unit plans and daily lessons (Titsworth et al., 2015).
- **Enhanced Instructional Design:** Alignment supports developing and organizing well-structured lessons and instructional materials, maximizing teaching strategies (Titsworth et al., 2015).
- **Improved Assessment Strategies:** Alignment helps develop assessments that accurately gauge student learning aligned with lesson instructional goals (Titsworth et al., 2015).
- **Targeted Interventions:** Better alignment allows teachers to precisely identify where specific students or groups struggle, facilitating targeted interventions (Schildkamp et al., 2020).

Benefits for Students:

- **Clear Learning Goals:** Alignment provides students with clear learning goals, helping them better understand learning expectations (Van Yperen et al., 2015).
- **Consistency in Learning:** Aligned instruction provides a coherent learning experience, reducing confusion and improving knowledge and skills retention (Van Yperen et al., 2015).
- **Increased Engagement:** Students tend to be more engaged when instruction is explicit, relevant, and directly tied to their learning goals (Wong et al., 2024).
- **Improved Achievement:** Well-aligned instruction is linked to improved academic performance and student outcomes (Van Yperen et al., 2015).

Due to these benefits, both a planning tool for mapping instruction backward (Valenzuela, 2022g) and a facilitation structure (Valenzuela, 2023) can help maintain alignment no matter what we encounter on an instructional day. The remainder of this chapter outlines how teaching teams can help promote instructional alignment in daily teaching within their schools using these tools.

Embracing Instructional Alignment Through Backward Design

When I began teaching, colleagues always encouraged me to map my lessons backward, but at that time, I didn't know anyone who could explain it in ways that made sense to me. The concept of planning lessons beginning with the end in mind made total sense in theory but was unattainable in practice. Seeking modeling and examples, I pursued professional development and eventually adapted a powerful tool for aligning my instruction (see Table 4.1) in 2014. A blank reproducible version of this table is available in Appendix A (page 155). As I practiced using the tool, alignment developed within my lessons.

TABLE 4.1: INSTRUCTIONAL ALIGNMENT TOOL

PRODUCT(S) AND TASKS Includes presentations, performance tasks, and summative assessments	LEARNING INTENTIONS AND PACING Includes knowledge, understanding, and skills required by students to complete products and tasks successfully	FORMATIVE ASSESSMENTS Includes both formal and informal checks of understanding to ensure students are on track with learning intentions	LESSONS, HIGH-YIELDING STRATEGIES, AND SCAFFOLDS Includes learning experiences that are closely aligned to learning intentions and formative assessments
Passion to Purpose 5-Step Organizer* (3–4 Class Periods)	I can examine and identify my passions and interests following the directions in my 5-step organizer (Valenzuela, 2022k). (1–2 class periods)	• Written reflection on 5-step organizer • Responses during classroom discussions • Exit ticket	• Teacher-led mini-lesson explaining major concepts • Videos explaining passion and providing service to others • Introduction to Passion to Purpose 5-Step Organizer • All-class discussion and debrief
	I can organize my findings and evidence in my 5-step organizer to support my passion and interests. (2 class periods)	• Written reflection on 5-step organizer • Feedback protocol using rubric • Checklist • Exit ticket	• Teacher directions and guiding questions • Passion to Purpose 5-Step Organizer • Teacher/student feedback

PRODUCT(S) AND TASKS Includes presentations, performance tasks, and summative assessments	LEARNING INTENTIONS AND PACING Includes knowledge, understanding, and skills required by students to complete products and tasks successfully	FORMATIVE ASSESSMENTS Includes both formal and informal checks of understanding to ensure students are on track with learning intentions	LESSONS, HIGH-YIELDING STRATEGIES, AND SCAFFOLDS Includes learning experiences that are closely aligned to learning intentions and formative assessments
	I can organize my content in my 5-step organizer effectively to ensure clarity and accuracy about solving a problem(s) of practice for a specific person or entity. (1 class period)	• Teacher-led discussion • Written explanation • Feedback protocol using rubric • Checklist • Exit ticket	• Teacher directions and guiding questions • Additional resources pertaining to specific problem(s) • Passion to Purpose 5-Step Organizer • Teacher/student feedback
	I can identify an expert(s) who can mentor and coach me as I build expertise to solve a problem of practice. (1 class period)	• Written reflection on 5-step organizer • Discussion with teacher • Exit ticket	• Individual and small-group teaching • Additional resources pertaining to specific expert(s) • Teacher/student feedback • Passion to Purpose 5-Step Organizer
	I can communicate what self-awareness means and how it pertains to making myself happy and fulfilled. (1 class period)	• Teacher-led discussion • Written and oral explanation • Poster presentation	• Working in pairs • Poster template • Teacher/student feedback • Passion to Purpose 5-Step Organizer

SOURCE: Inspired by Wiggins and McTighe, (2005)

***NOTE:** To access the Passion to Purpose 5-Step Organizer (Valenzuela, 2022k), visit https://wpvip.edutopia.org/wp-content/uploads/2023/01/PBL_Passion_to_Purpose_Planner-2.pdf

What's best is that I began intentionally planning for student engagement, identifying where I could initiate engagement strategies within lessons. Improved alignment in my lessons positively impacted my students' engagement and academic performance. They started to view the daily learning goal as a trusted guide for completing their daily tasks, consistently keeping them on track, and transforming into a personal affirmation of "I can . . ." after successful learning. Witnessing this breakthrough in my instructional practice was encouraging and significantly boosted my confidence in my teaching abilities.

I keep using it and improve my practice when a tool works well for me. For the past decade, backward design methodology has become a permanent component of my instructional design process, and many of the schools I work with have even added the tool to their lesson and performance task templates. See a template and completed example in Appendix A (pages 155 and 159). For many of the teaching teams I worked with, the tool has given them similar clarity and a better understanding of the curriculum mapping process. At times during the ideation process, we must stop to refresh our understanding of assessment, rewriting standards into learning goals and instructional scaffolds. I love seeing them make those valuable connections.

Mapping Instruction: A Planning Tool for Alignment

Backward design, also referred to as *backward mapping* or *backward planning*, is an instructional design process educators can use to develop logical teaching progressions in lessons, units of study, and courses. The central premise is to begin with the end in mind by stating the desired goals and outcomes for students, then work backward to identify and develop the appropriate assessments, learning experiences, instructional strategies, and scaffolds to achieve the outcomes (R. S. Bowen, 2017).

Having a planning tool and framework for mapping instruction backward can help teachers maintain alignment no matter what they encounter in the instructional day. The tool in Table 4.1 is inspired by Grant Wiggins and Jay McTighe's (2005) backward design methodology.

As mentioned in the previous section, I used it to clarify my instructional alignment and eventually reenvisioned it to fit my instructional design and teaching style. The tool does not replace Wiggins and McTighe's (2005) *Understanding by Design* resources and professional development through ASCD (n.d.). Instead, it is a simple four-column design that allows teachers to expertly map their instruction in alignment with summative assessment and daily learning goals.

Column 1: Establish Summative Assessment

When summative assessments align with standards or benchmarks, they drive instruction. Summative assessments can be products students create, demonstrations of performance tasks, final exams, end-of-term papers or essays, state-mandated assessments, portfolios showcasing student work, and culminating projects or presentations. For example, a specific unit or project plan may require students to create written, technology-based, or technology-constructed products such as reports, public service announcements, and model prototypes. The first step is determining what your students must accomplish and produce within a specific time frame. That information goes in column 1.

Column 2: Compose Learning Goals and Determine Pacing

Developing learning intentions for projects is a critical practice often neglected in professional development and, therefore, is often excluded or not well thought out in curriculum design. Derived from academic standards and learning frameworks, learning intentions are vital to teaching and observing learning and are the backbone of lessons. Good learning intentions drive what students will understand and what they will be able to accomplish following a lesson or project.

They must go beyond the objectives we need to meet in a particular lesson plan. They should be unpacked during mini-lessons as the focal point of the academic conversation between teachers and students. We suggest using learning intentions to capture learning goals as statements about what students can do regarding completing the summative assessment in column 1 of the alignment tool. You should also pace how long it will take your learners to master each of the learning intentions.

Column 3: Develop Formative Assessments

Each learning goal in column 2 will need formative assessment to check how well students are learning the material. Teachers can decide on both informal and formal formative assessments (Formplus, n.d.). Conducting two formal checks (quizzes, essays, etc.) for each summative assessment is a good practice for determining where students need help, remediation, and challenge. Informal checks can be used daily between our interactions with students to determine their instructional needs. Here are two common informal quick checks we can use daily to determine students' understanding.

- **Hand Signals:** Students giving a thumbs-up indicates they grasped the content enough to continue working, and a thumbs-down shows they need more time or further assistance understanding the material. Students who prefer privacy can discreetly hold their hand only in plain sight of their teacher (e.g., close to their chest).
- **Entry and Exit Slips:** Check-ins at the start and end of class can be used by teachers to gauge which part of the learning their students retained and where they are still stuck. Entry slips can be a question about the previous day of learning. Exit slips are provided at the end of class to inform teachers about student progress and where upcoming lessons need to focus. Here are some adaptable prompts teachers can use for slips.
  - What two things have you learned well, and what are you still struggling to understand?
  - What interests you most about what you're learning in class?
  - What did you find most difficult about today's lesson?

Column 4: Mini-Lessons and Utilizing High-Yielding Strategies and Scaffolds

Educators can use mini-lessons (shorter lessons) to ensure daily lessons cater to all students, granting more time for individual and group work and reteaching lessons in smaller groups (TeacherVision, n.d.). These shorter lesson formats can introduce new concepts and daily learning goals, providing a platform for modeling new strategies and discussing assigned tasks (TeacherVision, 2019; Valenzuela, 2023). Mini-lessons can effectively ignite interest, prompt student inquiries, and actively engage learners when facilitated well.

High-yielding strategies and scaffolds are what we reach for to teach a particular lesson—in this case, the learning intention(s) in column 2. Learning intentions require teachers to explain, clarify, and model (Valenzuela, 2023). Students will need time to practice moving from guided (teacher-led) to independent learning. Use the information in building block 3 of the previous chapter on page 48 to determine what makes a strategy high-yielding, and select appropriate ones teachers can use to teach their lessons for each learning intention.

Gleaning insights from formative assessment (column 2) helps teachers put the appropriate scaffolds and interventions in place by updating column 4. For example, to help students with particular skills, we like structuring their learning using station rotations, allowing them to move between working independently and with the teacher or their peers. Teachers can also use a similar process for differentiating and choosing scaffolds that work best for their students. Common scaffolds may include but are not limited to the following (Houser, n.d.):

- **Teacher modeling:** Through demonstrations, teachers show students how to complete a task or activity and provide insights into the thought processes of its completion.
- **Sentence stems** are excellent scaffolds for helping learners explain their thoughts and ideas. Sentence stems can be a powerful support for English language learners (ELLs). Here are some that we recommend:
    - The paragraph states the following: . . .
    - Overall, what the author is trying to say is . . .
    - I disagree with their position because . . .
    - I do not understand what the author meant by . . . in the second paragraph. Can you please help clarify?
- **Graphic organizers:** This visual and graphic display tool created by students depicts the relationships between facts, terms, and ideas within learning a major and vital concept(s). Graphic organizers come in many forms (hierarchical sets, descriptive or thematic maps, flow charts, etc.).
- **Connect to previous knowledge:** When planning mini-lessons, teachers can consider students' background knowledge about a concept they can connect to. For example, you can show them a picture or text related to their new learning and ask them if they have any prior experience with the topic.
- **Use of first language:** If your ELLs' first language can improve learning the content you teach, use it as a scaffold. Only translate parts of lessons such as essential vocabulary words, concept connections, and step-by-step task instructions.

Mapping Instruction Simplified Using Artificial Intelligence

As you now know, the instructional alignment tool in Table 4.1 is powerful for mapping our daily teaching. However, there's more than one way to skin a cat. New artificial intelligence (AI) developments enable teachers to leverage AI capabilities through innovative apps like ChatGPT and Microsoft Copilot to streamline mapping instruction. That's right: doing the same thing but faster! AI technology can be leveraged as a knowledgeable personal assistant—you should consider using it. I now leverage AI tools in my collaborative curriculum mapping sessions, and teachers love it!

Generative AI is one current iteration of AI with the power to create new high-quality content—including images, code, video, and text—by learning from patterns in existing sources (Zewe, 2023). You can complete the instructional alignment tool (see Table 4.1) by following along with me in a video (Flip, 2024) where I explain completing the activity step by step. I recommend watching each part of the video while pausing, as needed, to practice independently. Feel free to edit the prompts I provided to align and map lessons to fit your lesson context.

Transitioning to Applied Instructional Strategies

Teaching teams can leverage the knowledge discussed thus far in this chapter to help the teachers they serve align daily instruction. Furthermore, it gives teachers lots to consider about their lesson planning and overall instructional design practices for teaching and learning. A lot goes into becoming a skilled curriculum developer and facilitator of knowledge—it does not happen overnight. To begin developing their pedagogical strategies for planning and facilitating, we hope the systematic approach of using tools and frameworks is empowering because of the repetitiveness of it all. Now that we know how to align daily instruction, let's pay attention to how mapped lessons can be facilitated using a complementary systematic approach to what we just learned.

Building Teacher Self-Efficacy for Daily Teaching

Chapter 3 (page 43) covered building teacher self-efficacy using timely feedback. Now, we are focusing on self-efficacy within the context of daily teaching. This is vital because teaching team leaders should always strive to improve their teachers' self-efficacy and overall teaching confidence. Research suggests that developing self-efficacy is an internal motivational process that can be positively influenced by a collaborative and supportive school environment. Factors contributing to this include positive interactions with colleagues, administrative support, peer mentoring, and personalized feedback (Valenzuela, 2022b; Woolfolk & Hoy, 1990).

In a seminal study, professors Megan Tschannen-Moran, PhD, and Anita Woolfolk Hoy, PhD, examined the relationship between teacher self-efficacy and instructional strategies. Findings showed that teachers with increased beliefs in their abilities used more innovative teaching practices, improving student academic achievement (Tschannen-Moran & Hoy, 2001). Therefore, when co-creating professional development experiences with our partner schools, we aim to nurture community and sound teaching by meeting colleagues where they are in their teaching journey after observing instruction in real time.

The top focus areas for teaching teams should be beginning teachers and those needing refreshers on the aspects of instruction that require strong self-efficacy and time to build and are crucial for daily teaching. Many of these elements are addressed in the initial chapters of this book—which may include effective core instruction (Valenzuela, 2022c), instructional alignment (Valenzuela, 2022g), student engagement (Valenzuela, 2022e), and differentiation strategies (Valenzuela, 2023). Your team should aim to build capacity in these critical areas to help grow your teachers into confident, skilled educators (Sackstein, 2016).

A Powerful Structure for Daily Teaching

While conducting instructional rounds (Valenzuela, 2024a), we see many instances of overreliance on direct instruction and students completing worksheets during work time. We will delve into instructional rounds in Chapter 6 (page 87). In my school district, I (Serbrenia) have seen that a combination of COVID-19 decimating instruction and the current teacher shortage has contributed to folks entering teaching from nontraditional pathways (e.g., career switchers and newbies to education during the pandemic), causing a disconnect between research-informed teaching and instructional innovation (Valenzuela, 2023). They hold classes five days a week—our current charge is to move beyond direct instruction and build their confidence for daily instruction!

Teaching teams know there is no perfect or only way to teach, but many teachers need a starting point. Drawing inspiration from Samantha Bennett's (2007) teaching structure, we developed a visual for helping teachers outline how they can structure their daily learning block. We found this powerful for helping them understand the role of direct instruction to help set up differentiation during work time in their daily teaching. Please see Figure 4.1.

The following sections share ways we developed to build teachers' self-efficacy by immediately providing them with ideas for structure during their teaching block and differentiation strategies (Valenzuela, 2023). Attention to this will allow teachers overly dependent on direct instruction to consider adding other strategies to their

FIGURE 4.1: ADAPTATION OF SAMANTHA BENNETT'S TEACHING STRUCTURE FOR DAILY TEACHING

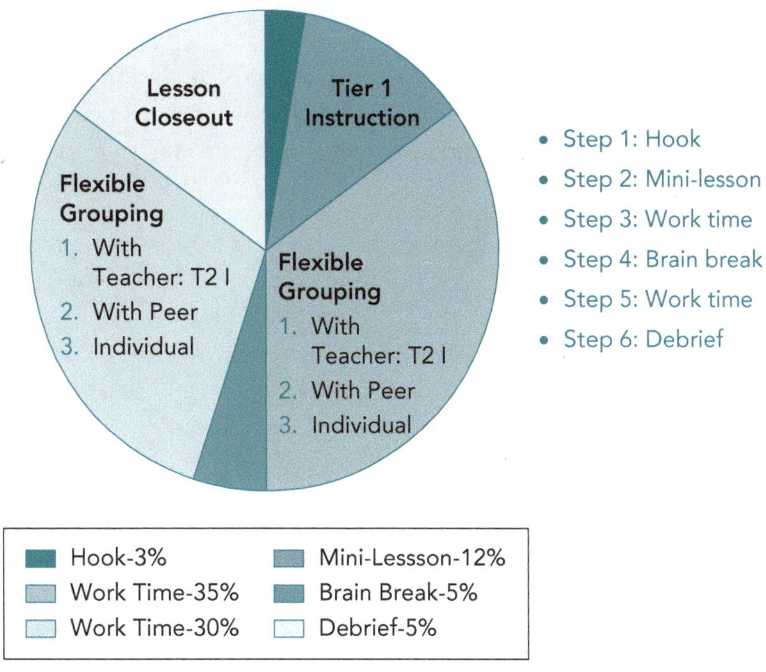

SOURCE: Adapted from Bennett, 2007.

teaching. We recommend that teaching teams model and practice these tasks during common planning time, teaching team meetings, and districtwide in-service days.

Here is a practical breakdown.

Direct Instruction

After an engaging lesson hook, direct instruction in a mini-lesson is a powerful tool for providing learners with the intended learning context, setting the tone for the remainder of the learning block. Here are four steps teachers can take in 10–15 minutes (see Figure 4.2).

1. **Unpack the daily learning goal(s).** Both elementary and secondary learners will need help on the front end of the learning block to understand the purpose of the intended learning articulated in the learning goal. Teachers' taking time to help them make sense of new vocabulary—including the nouns (what they are learning) and the verbs (what they will be doing)—leads to smoother sailing. Younger learners (K–2) will need more scaffolding, more explanation, and less text-heavy learning targets.

2. **Clarify any misconceptions.** Vague or incorrect understanding leads to barriers in learning, especially for learners with weak prior knowledge. Taking time to gauge, explain, clarify, and allow learners to ask questions is crucial for helping teachers understand where students need assistance before moving forward.
3. **Practice teacher modeling (I do, we do, you do).** Before learners are unleashed to work, they must clearly understand what they are aiming for. Modeling by the teacher on the front end is a helpful way to shift learning responsibilities gradually.
4. **Clearly define work time.** Teachers should explain logistics, grouping, and other essential information students need before working individually or in groups.

Figure 4.2 is a quick guide for what needs to happen during direct instruction.

FIGURE 4.2: QUICK GUIDE FOR DIRECT INSTRUCTION

1. Unpacking the Learning Goal(s)
2. Clarifying Misconceptions
3. Modeling (I do, we do, you do)
4. Setting up the work time portion of the learning block

Flexible and Individual Grouping: A Model for Differentiated Instruction

When students consistently passively sit, complete worksheets, or socialize during work, it is a missed learning opportunity. Flexible grouping is a research-informed method of temporarily grouping students with varying skill levels to achieve learning goals through collaboration and guided instruction (Morin, n.d.). When used correctly, it gets students to speak using academic language associated with the learning goal unpacked during the mini-lesson. Teachers can organize flexible groupings using the following format (see Figure 4.3):

1. Work with the teacher or a paraprofessional.
2. Work with a peer(s).
3. Work individually.

Some of our partner schools use this strategy to implement Tier 2 and 3 interventions. See Figures 4.3 and 4.4 for a list of strategies for each of the three categories. Figure 4.3 represents a comprehensive collection of strategies, while Figure 4.4 offers a more manageable and practical starting point for teachers new to flexible grouping. Using ChatGPT, we defined all of the strategies teachers can consider employing for their groups (to the best of our ability, we edited this list to remove inaccurate material).

FIGURE 4.3: COMPREHENSIVE COLLECTION OF STRATEGIES FOR FLEXIBLE GROUPING

TEACHER- AND PARA-LED WORK (TIERS 2 AND 3)	STUDENT-LED WORK	INDEPENDENT WORK
• Differentiated Instruction • Skill Remediation • Guided Practice • Discussion and Questioning • Assessment and Feedback • Socratic Seminars • Literacy Circles • Project Planning and Collaboration • Language Development • Feedback on Assignments • Skill-Based Rotation • Monitoring Process • Extension and Enrichment	• Collaborative Learning • Peer Teaching • Discussion and Debate • Research and Inquiry • Problem Solving • Peer Editing and Feedback • Project Planning and Management • Peer Assessment • Role Assignments • Reflection • Peer Support • STEM Projects	• Reading • Research Projects • Journaling • Creative Writing • Math Practice • Art Projects • Science Experiments • Coding and Programming • Language Learning • Music Practice • Personal Projects • Critical Thinking Activities • Volunteer Work • Online Learning Platforms • Portfolios

FIGURE 4.4: STRATEGIES FOR FLEXIBLE GROUPING

TEACHER- AND PARA-LED WORK (TIERS 2 AND 3)	STUDENT-LED WORK	INDEPENDENT WORK
• Differentiated Instruction • Skill Remediation • Guided Practice • Discussion and Questioning • Assessments and Feedback • Literacy Circles • Language Development • Feedback on Assignments	• Peer Support and Collaboration • Modified Role Assignments	• Reading • Journaling • Mathematics Practice • Art Projects • Language Learning • Volunteer Work • Online Learning Platforms • Portfolios

Teachers new to flexible grouping may find that executing this strategy logistically may be clunky initially but becomes smoother with time and practice. Building self-efficacy for you and students who are engaging using the format can be developed through consistent implementation. Remember to give students a brain break (especially younger ones). This can be done about midway through the specified chunk of work time (see Figure 4.1).

Lesson Closeout and Debrief

How teachers close lessons is just as important as how they begin them. Be intentional by revisiting the learning goal and quickly checking in to hear student reflections and takeaways. Other powerful ways to end lessons may include one-word shares (Boryga, 2023), low-stakes quizzes, and quick reviews (Finley, 2015). Exit tickets are another great way to end lessons and get students thinking metacognitively about their learning, participation, and how well their teacher's instruction engaged and assisted them with learning. This form of student feedback can help build teachers' self-efficacy for the new strategies they are learning to facilitate well. Some good exit prompts may include the following (Facing History and Ourselves, 2023):

- What three things did you learn from today's lesson?
- Evaluate your participation and collaboration with others today. What are two things you did really well, and what will you improve next time?
- What can I do better in future lessons to help you learn and be better engaged?

See Figure 4.5 for a downloadable flexible and individual grouping plan for a lesson.

FIGURE 4.5: FLEXIBLE AND INDIVIDUAL GROUPING PLAN

Teacher- or Para-Led Lesson	Peer-Led Lesson	Independent Lesson
Description: *Students are arranged into small groups based on their unique learning needs, fostering tailored instruction and collaboration for improved outcomes.*	***Description:*** *Students are grouped into small teams to achieve targeted objectives/tasks, promoting collaboration, with one student taking on a leadership position, while the group actively participates in academic discussions.*	***Description:*** *Students engage in independent tasks tailored to their unique strengths, interests, and learning goals, ensuring personalized attention and self-paced progress to address individualized needs.*

Strategies	Strategies	Strategies
• Differentiated Instruction ☐ • Skill Remediation ☐ • Guided Practice ☐ • Discussion and Questioning ☐ • Assessment and Feedback ☐ • Literacy Circles ☐ • Language Development ☐ • Feedback on Assignments ☐	• Peer Support and Collaboration Stations ☐ • Modified Role Assignments ☐	• Reading ☐ • Journaling ☐ • Mathematics Practice ☐ • Art Projects ☐ • Language Learning ☐ • Volunteer Work ☐ • Online Learning Platforms ☐ • Portfolios ☐

Please see an explanation of the strategies in Appendix A (page 162).

Chapter Summary

This chapter delved into the crucial aspects of instructional alignment and daily teaching. We provided practical tools that teaching team leaders can use to help their teachers synchronize their daily teaching, such as student learning goals, teaching strategies, and assessments. Beginning with backward design methodology, we emphasized the importance of coherence in planning daily lessons. We introduced and modeled the use of a planning tool that guides teachers in aligning their instruction with summative assessment, learning goals, formative assessments, high-yielding teaching strategies, and instructional scaffolds.

We also emphasized the need to build teacher self-efficacy for teaching, providing insights into building confidence through collaborative environments and structuring daily teaching. By emphasizing structured instructional strategies like direct instruction, flexible grouping, and good lesson closeouts, this chapter (Chapter 4) aims to empower teaching team leaders in helping teachers implement sound teaching strategies, fostering a coherent and purposeful learning experience for students across various subjects. Furthermore, this chapter serves as the culmination of a unified path toward instructional innovation, serving as foundational learning, understanding, and practice teaching team leaders can harness for true instructional innovation in their school using the action research model introduced in Part II of this book.

Reflective Prompts for Individual Teaching Team Members

1. Consider your previous understanding of instructional alignment for daily teaching. Which concepts affirmed or challenged you most as you learned alignment within the context of backward design as explained in this chapter? How might you begin implementing the alignment tool in your curriculum mapping?
2. Reflect on the teachers your teaching team currently serves. What can you do to help them align their daily lessons? How can you improve their self-efficacy for daily teaching using sound instructional strategies such as direct instruction and flexible grouping?
3. Envision your entire school on the same page about instructional alignment and structure for daily teaching. Consider the impact of good instructional alignment on students. What can you do right now to make positive strides toward helping your teaching team make this a reality?

Reflective Prompts for Teaching Teams

1. As a teaching team, discuss instructional alignment for mapping daily teaching. How can the teaching team begin helping the teachers they serve to develop their understanding and practices around alignment?
2. Discuss how teachers at your school implement direct instruction and group work. What steps will the teaching team take to ensure that teachers understand the roles of direct instruction and group work in their daily teaching? How will the Teaching Team improve the teaching staff's understanding of these insights?
3. Visualize how the teaching team wishes teachers to apply instructional alignment in their daily teaching. What must be in place to facilitate this understanding amongst the teaching staff, and can it benefit students? How will teaching team leaders prepare themselves to help teachers achieve the desired levels of implementation?

Part II

Five Steps to Instructional Innovation Through Action Research

After Part I laid a solid foundation for instructional innovation by addressing building collaborative teams, establishing effective feedback, delivering effective core instruction, and aligning instruction and assessment, Part II of this book now introduces the 5-Step Instructional Innovation Model for teaching teams to achieve instructional innovation through action research. Through this model, readers will learn how to collaboratively solve instructional problems by visiting classrooms to observe teaching to identify instruction areas needing improvement, capture desired outcomes, and analyze data to determine growth areas. The model emphasizes visiting classrooms, collaborative discussions, alignment with existing practices, and utilizing data-driven insights to inform future professional development solutions. By following these steps, instructional leaders and teachers can effectively address instructional challenges, enhance teaching practices, and drive meaningful improvements in their schools.

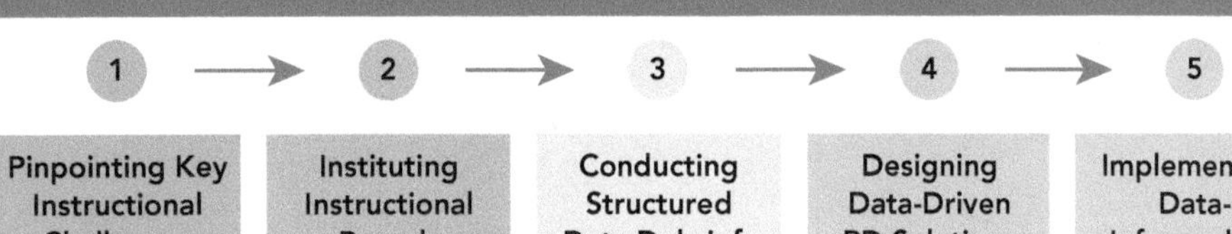

Beginning with core instruction, teaching teams identify key instructional challenges in their school or district.	Teaching teams conduct learning walks in schools to observe instruction and collect data related to the area(s) identified in Step 1.	Teaching teams establish guidelines for unpacking and level-setting the data collected during instructional rounds in Step 2.	Teaching teams create data-driven professional development (PD) interventions by prioritizing the solutions identified in Step 3.	After delivering PD, teaching teams collect relevant data from participants to evaluate effectiveness of the prescribed interventions.

CHAPTER 5

Step 1: Pinpointing Key Instructional Challenges and Problems of Practice

This chapter discusses ways teaching teams can identify and address critical instructional challenges and problems of practice in schools or districts. Since teachers are the instructional backbone of schools, ways of leveraging their expertise and involving them in the decision-making process are discussed to lead the process. Additionally, we begin providing a step-by-step guide for carrying out instructional innovation using an action research process and methodology teaching teams can use to craft a strong problem statement that clearly outlines the issue and desired outcomes. We'll also focus on defining specific areas of instruction that need improvement—using classroom culture, core instruction and differentiation as examples. Finally, we stress the importance of documenting desired outcomes, including observable behaviors and classroom culture. By following the guidance in this chapter, instructional leaders and teachers can work together to begin effectively addressing instructional challenges and improving site-based teaching practices.

Carefully Selecting Your Teaching Team—Including Teachers

Selecting your teaching team members is not solely about gathering a group of educators—it is about assembling a team of visionaries and collaborators devoted to their school's transformation. As Stephen Covey (2020) discusses in *The 7 Habits of Highly Effective People*, a team of people is not merely people working together but a collective synergizing on a shared vision and mission. Team building does not happen by accident—it must be orchestrated.

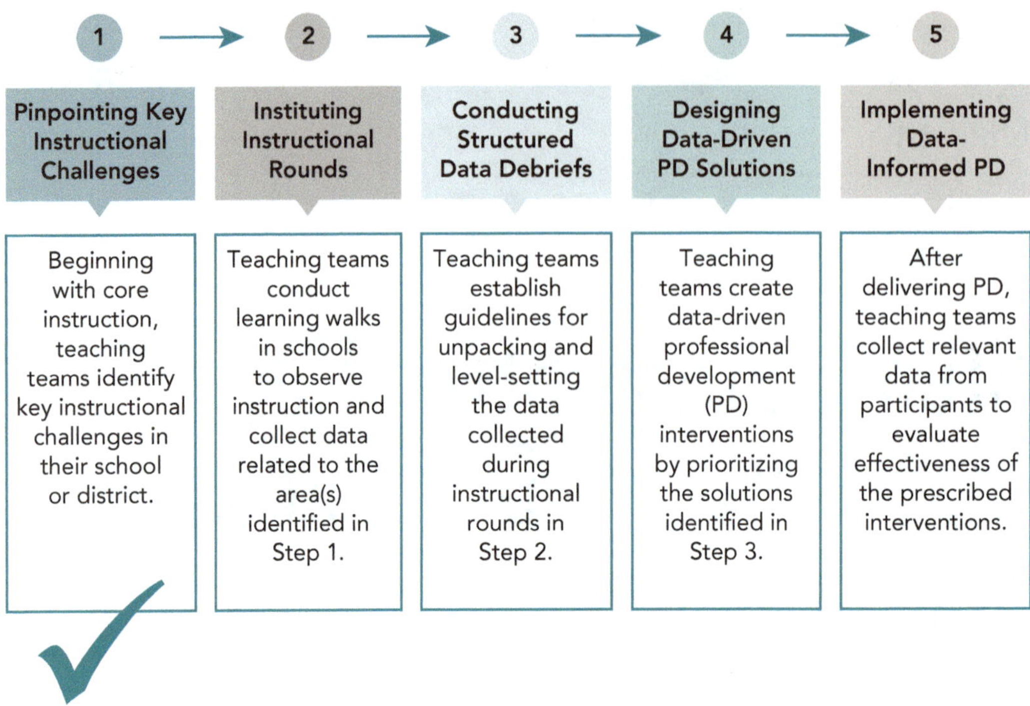

There is extensive research to support the pivotal role team member selection and recruitment may play in shaping the trajectory of sustained instructional progress (Darling-Hammond et al., 2017; Johnson, 2016). When assembling your school's teaching team, include folks responsible for improving instruction—such as assistant principals, lead teachers, instructional coaches, and teachers from various disciplines and content areas. The following considerations are crucial to sustained success over the long haul:

1. **Utilizing Teachers to Help Drive Collective Efficacy:** Research affirms that involving key stakeholders in decision making significantly enhances the efficacy and sustainability of implemented strategies (Bernat et al., 2023; Huang, 2023). In the action research model outlined in this book's section, teacher representation on the teaching team is the cornerstone of this equation. Including teachers is not symbolic; it is foundational for gaining credibility and earning the respect and buy-in from the entire faculty. They are still in classrooms and can offer invaluable insights needed for implementation. Discussions, decisions, and instructional innovation initiatives about teaching approaches and professional development must reflect their experiences and insights.
2. **Championing Personal and Professional Transformation:** Successful teaching teams consist of individuals with an unwavering commitment to transforming both themselves and their school. Instructional innovation is a journey that demands a collective resolve to challenge conventional paradigms, embrace change, continuously evolve, and build capacity for common

professional practices (Kunnari et al., 2017). In assembling a teaching team, leaders must identify team members who see transformation as a dynamic, ongoing process rather than a static outcome.

3. **Commitment to Action Research:** Addressing instructional challenges within schools requires a holistic and systemic approach based on data collection and practical insights derived from action research. Commitment to engaging in action research to improve instructional problems can enhance the teaching environment and help teachers solve students' problems (Albalawi & Johnson, 2022). For this to work, the teaching team must commit to collectively engaging in classroom observations, rigorous data analysis, and collaborative problem solving. The action research model outlined in this section provides the compass for guiding interventions that teams can actively use to seek evidence-driven solutions personalized to their school's unique context.

All in all, the alchemy of an effective teaching team isn't because of the amalgam of titles of its members. Teams thrive in the intersections of diverse perspectives, unwavering dedication to transformation, and a shared commitment to data-informed, systemic improvement. Your school's teachers must see themselves represented by decision makers, and their interests must be valued. Leaders who realize the power of collective efficacy can foster a culture where each team member believes their voice is heard and is used to shape instructional innovation to yield positive results (Sánchez-Rosas et al., 2022).

Using Action Research to Address Instructional Problems of Practice

Action research is a systematic inquiry process educators can conduct within their own school context to solve specific instructional problems of practice, improve how they implement strategies, and enhance student academic outcomes (Mertler, 2021). The action research process can help teaching teams connect theory and practice by engaging together in iterative cycles of inquiry, research, planning, observing, implementing, collecting data, and reflecting (Mertler, 2021). In our practice, we have found this process critical for learning new practices and how to implement them, along with inspecting to see how they work within our specific contexts.

Documentation is critical to the action research process, ensuring transparency, task accountability, and the systematic progression of the instructional innovation carried out by teaching teams (Bridges, 2024). Utilizing project management tools such as an action plan is necessary for teaching teams to record professional development (PD) interventions, barriers, and solutions to instructional problems; specify team members' roles; and establish timelines (Holzer, 2024). Think of your team's action plan as a structured framework in a document identifying and clarifying the path toward the desired outcomes.

To get your team started on developing and updating your plans, beginning with the problem statement, we created an action plan document you can download in Appendix A (page 172). You may use the template to begin mapping your initial problem statement. Further guidance on using the action plan document will be outlined in the subsequent chapters in this section.

Rationale for Crafting Problem Statements

The first step in action research is crafting a solid problem statement—serving as a compass for navigating the research process (McCombes & George, 2023). Readers who have participated in a graduate program and created a research design will understand what we mean in this section regarding problem statements. Others may require further explanation. The problem statement helps clarify the problem of practice, define the desired outcomes, and delineate the scope of the inquiry (Wrike Team, 2024). A well-defined problem statement sets the course for focused, purposeful action and gathering relevant data to inform the next steps and solutions (McCombes & George, 2023; Wrike Team, 2024).

Step-by-Step Guide to Crafting Problem Statements

A good problem statement sets the stage for successful action research and guides the teaching team toward data-informed solutions tailored to their specific teaching context. We recommend teaching teams co-create and revise actionable and realistic problem statements. Here are some helpful steps and examples to help you get started.

1. **Identify the Problem Area:** Start by pinpointing a specific instructional challenge or area needing improvement within the team's school or a particular classroom setting. Feel free to dig deeper and conduct a comprehensive needs assessment. This may include reviewing data from student performance assessments and classroom observations and gathering feedback from your pertinent stakeholders, such as teachers and students. Prioritize the identified areas based on their significance to student learning outcomes.

2. **Clarify the Issue:** Articulate the problem by describing its impact on student learning, the school environment, and culture. To ensure each team member fully comprehends impacts, provide specific examples depicting how the identified problem area(s) manifests in classrooms and school environments. Also, consider incorporating relevant research findings or educational literature to deepen understanding of the problem's implications.

3. **Define Desired Outcomes:** Outline the desired changes and improvements the team wants as a result of addressing the problem. These outcomes should be observable, measurable, and aligned to the teaching team's goals. As the

team brainstorms, use concrete language to articulate the specific behaviors, skills, or attitudes everyone desires to foster in teachers and students by addressing the identified problem. Describe how the desired outcomes will be observed and measured and provide examples of assessment tools (e.g., rubrics and performance tasks) the team will use to gauge progress toward success.

4. **Consider Contextual Factors:** Factor in the unique context of the school or classroom when framing the problem statement. Consider factors such as student readiness and engagement and demographics, available resources, and current instructional practices. Consider how they may impact the implementation and effectiveness of interventions. Conjure up solutions that nurture collaboration among key stakeholders, such as teachers, students, administrators, and community members, toward eliminating barriers.
5. **Narrow Scope and Focus:** Make sure the problem statement is straightforward and manageable and that the team agrees to work on it. Avoid overly broad statements that might confuse the focus and research process. Be sure to engage in discussions and reflection to ensure team consensus on the problem statement's scope. Seek and provide guidance on refining the problem statement to be measurable. This can be accomplished by breaking it into smaller components to facilitate focused research and intervention.

Additionally, as your team collects data and answers questions that lead to new questions, you will discover the iterative nature of action research and problem statements. Your problem statements might evolve as the team progresses through the action research cycle. Refining or adjusting them based on new insights or findings is completely normal and acceptable.

Crafting Problem Statements and Defining Instructional Goals: Classroom Examples

In the earlier chapters of this book, we discussed the importance of school and classroom culture, having foundational core instruction, and utilizing differentiation strategies during lessons. Let's explore classroom scenarios for each of these topics in elementary, middle, and high school settings and create a breakdown showing a clear problem statement, define the area of instruction improvement, and outline the desired outcomes for each.

Classroom Culture

Problem Statement

In a fourth-grade classroom, there is a noticeably subdued culture due to limited student participation and engagement during routine classroom activities, leading to minimal collaboration among students during group work.

Area of Instruction Improvement

The team aims to enhance student participation and engagement by using strategies that promote positive student interactions during classroom activities by fostering a classroom culture that encourages active engagement and collaboration.

Components of Improvement

- Implement high-yielding strategies that influence student engagement to promote active participation and involvement during group tasks.
- Cultivate a classroom culture that values participation during classroom activities and encourages student collaboration.

Desired Outcomes

- Increased student engagement and active participation during all activities, including group work with peers.
- Improved collaboration skills, fostering a more cohesive and engaged classroom environment.

Core Instruction

Problem Statement

There is a significant number of middle school students who are struggling with algebraic concepts, indicating a gap in understanding the fundamental principles that are necessary for sequential coursework and future academic mathematical pursuits.

Area of Instruction Improvement

The team aims to enhance the teaching of algebraic concepts to provide middle school students with a strong foundation for current academic success and future academic pursuits in mathematics.

Components of Improvement

- Develop and implement targeted lessons emphasizing foundational algebraic principles articulated via clear learning goals.
- Utilization of evidence-based instructional strategies with strong influences on student comprehension and mastery of key algebraic concepts.

Desired Outcomes

- Improved proficiency and mastery of the algebraic concepts students must possess to reinforce a solid foundation for higher-level mathematics courses.
- Increased confidence, preparedness, and motivation among students for advanced coursework and future academic endeavors in mathematics.

Differentiation of Instruction

Problem Statement

In several high school English language arts (ELA) classes with mixed levels, there is a challenge in meeting diverse reading needs specifically in comprehension levels, hindering the ability to effectively deliver tailored instruction for every student.

Area of Instruction Improvement

The team aims to implement instructional strategies that personalize learning experiences for students with varying reading comprehension levels.

Components of Improvement

- Implementation of various high-yielding instructional approaches, resources, and scaffolds to accommodate diverse reading comprehension levels within each of the classes.
- Utilization of assessment data to inform appropriate interventions, offering targeted support to students based on their individual learning needs.

Desired Outcomes

- Increased student engagement and motivation through more personalized instruction.
- Improved reading comprehension skills among students across varying ability levels, boosted academic achievement, and raised confidence in reading skills.

In postpandemic classrooms, culture, core instruction, and differentiation strategies are critical areas we believe teaching teams need to look at closely during instructional rounds (see Chapter 6, page 87). This is why we addressed them again in this section of the book—especially during the topic of developing problem statements. However, you may adapt and rewrite these in your own context or proceed differently. The suggested steps of articulating the instructional problem, area of instruction needing improvement, components of improvement, and desired outcome are vital steps in moving toward action research using the model in this section.

Collaborative Problem Solving Without Using a Problem Statement

As covered in the preceding sections, for complex instructional problems requiring extended time to solve, teaching teams can define them well and develop a problem statement as part of a 5-step action research model for instructional innovation (Valenzuela, 2022j). However, not every problem requires in-depth exploration or a lengthy timeline to determine and implement a viable solution(s).

Needing a simpler yet collaborative approach to solve issues that aren't overwhelmingly complex but are still challenging enough to require thoughtful consideration and creative thinking to solve, I developed an adaptation of the traditional Plus/Delta protocol (Lean Construction Institute, n.d.). We call the updated version the Plus, Delta, Solution (PDS) protocol. The PDS strategy emphasizes effective collaboration and communication as crucial aspects of problem solving within teams and in a manner where everyone on the teaching staff feels safe contributing.

We have implemented the PDS protocol with school and district leaders and achieved good results. Moreover, this protocol can help teaching teams identify challenges to student success, leverage strengths, and most importantly find solutions, all while promoting shared problem solving, which is currently needed in many schools. The protocol can also be modified for use with students during lessons and projects and to create social awareness for classroom problems like internet safety, digital citizenship, bullying, and social exclusion.

Before diving into the steps of the PDS strategy, here are four outcomes of how using the protocol can empower and benefit your teaching team:

1. **Promoting Structured Communication:** Drawing structured communication between colleagues creates a platform for everyone to share their ideas, observations, concerns, and solutions while keeping discussions focused. For instance, teaching teams can use this approach to solve instructional issues such as curriculum enhancements, behavioral management, and technology integration. Logistical problems such as resource allocation, timetabling and scheduling, and after-school event planning can also be tackled by teams through structured communication.
2. **Encouraging Diverse Perspectives:** Establishing norms and shared agreements (see Chapter 1, page 17) within the protocol can guarantee everyone who wants to will speak or contribute, ensuring different viewpoints are considered. This deliberate attention to inclusivity helps explore various angles to a problem and prevents tunnel vision.
3. **Creating Documentation and Review:** Using the protocol to document discussions, ideas, and solutions aids in tracking the team's suggestions, concerns, and decisions. Documented materials can also be reviewed later to

continue aligning goals and solutions and to avoid revisiting previously discussed points.

4. **Establishing Feedback and Reflection Mechanisms:** When the protocol incorporates mechanisms for both feedback and reflection, team members work together to refine thoughts, practice, and approaches to community problem solving. Doing so promotes a culture of learning and improvement throughout the school that can be transferred to students and other staff members.

Important Note for Facilitators of the PDS Protocol: The four steps outlined as follows can be carried out in approximately 26–40 minutes. Whether facilitating with colleagues or with students, feel free to customize and adapt directions and timings to serve the needs of your intended audience better. Additionally, see Appendix A (page 168) for some graphics you can use to guide implementation.

Step 1: Allow the Teaching Team to State the Problem (5–7 Minutes)

The purpose here is to arrive at a consensus for the problem the team will address in the subsequent steps of the protocol. Sometimes, everyone arrives knowing the issue that needs solving, and sometimes, the facilitator has to inquire. The PDS protocol can be opened up according to the team's needs in one of two ways: (1) If the problem is already agreed upon before commencing with the protocol, that is fantastic. If not, (2) provide question prompts that allow colleagues to speak freely.

We use some of these when introducing the protocol during faculty meetings or professional development.

1. "It's hard to focus on instruction when ___________ behavior is a constant concern."
2. "I'm having difficulty with a specific management task(s)."
3. "I'm struggling to keep up with the intended pacing in my lessons."
4. "I'm overwhelmed by a constant challenge."

Step 2: Individually Identify Pluses and Deltas Pertaining to the Problem (4 Minutes)

To promote a positive mindset toward problem solving while identifying the difficulties associated with the problem(s) and using small posted notes, each team member identifies pluses (what's working well) and deltas (the drawbacks, challenges, or areas that need improvement.). Request the team members not to focus on solutions in this step.

Step 3: Discuss the Pluses and Deltas Within Small Groups (7 Minutes)

To get everyone comfortable discussing their reflections from Step 2, adapt and provide the following directions and time for folks to communicate with team members.

1. Identify two grade-level colleagues to work with.
2. Collaborate to develop and complete a PDS Chart (see Appendix A, page 170) using your posted notes from Step 2. Avoid redundancy by discarding posted notes with similar text.
3. Have the teams discuss their pluses and deltas without focusing on solutions. Everyone needs to develop comfortability in discussing the deltas as they are.

Step 4: Begin to Develop Answers (15–20 Minutes)

This part of the protocol is intended to find appropriate solutions to the identified problem(s) through thoughtful reflection and consideration. Stress the importance of not offering concrete solutions to issues they haven't yet seen solved to team members. Sometimes guidance from an outside source or entity is needed, so further exploration by team members may be necessary. Display directions for this step using the following prompts.

1. On a posted note, offer a solution(s)/resource(s) to address the problem. Do this independently, and don't feel obliged to provide a solution if you don't have one. (5–10 minutes, depending on how many issues are being addressed)
2. Reconvene with your thought partners from Step 3 to discuss the solution(s) provided. (5 minutes)
3. Participate in reflection and open discussion with the entire team. (5 minutes)

We are well aware that problem solving isn't easy. Although it requires careful thought and consideration, it doesn't have to be stressful. Having a system like PDS, which focuses on solutions through collaboration, can really encourage your teaching team to see the value in working together to find answers.

Chapter Summary

This chapter delved into laying the groundwork for instructional innovation by having teaching team leaders carefully consider their team member selection—especially being intentional about representing teachers. After establishing teaching teams, practical ways of pinpointing the instructional challenges they may encounter within their educational settings were also covered. The importance and steps for crafting problem statements were provided, along with examples of topics previously covered in Part I of this book, such as classroom culture, core instruction, differentiation, and alignment.

We also provided detailed steps of the Plus, Delta, Solution (PDS) protocol as a collaborative problem-solving tool teams can use when there's no need to craft problem statements. Now that we know how to outline instructional problems, we are ready to navigate instructional rounds in Chapter 6, knowing precisely what we are looking for.

Reflective Prompts for Individual Teaching Team Members

1. Reflect on your previous understanding of action research. Which concepts affirmed or challenged you most as you learned about the importance of composing good problem statements? How might you introduce this practice to new members of your teaching team?
2. Consider the teachers your teaching team supports. What can you do to help them understand the role of action research in your school's instructional innovation process?
3. Envision your teaching team addressing a problem using the Plus, Delta, Solution (PDS) protocol for the very first time. How can you facilitate the protocol ensuring each member feels their contributions are valued?

Reflective Prompts for Teaching Teams

1. Within the teaching team, discuss action research for instructional innovation and needs assessment. How might the team begin crafting accurate problem statements to address identified need(s)?
2. Discuss the teaching team's past approach to instructional innovation. Was action research a part of the process? How will the teaching team ensure that each member understands the purpose of action research beginning with crafting problem statements, outlining components of improvement, and the desired outcomes?
3. Why may the teaching team implement the Plus, Delta, Solutions (PDS) protocol? What's needed to facilitate PDS effectively? How will teaching team leaders guide the protocol to achieve the outcome of collaborative problem solving?

CHAPTER 6

Step 2: Conducting Instructional Rounds Using Learning Walks

This chapter emphasizes the importance of conducting quarterly instructional rounds and frequent learning walks to observe instruction and collect data related to the problem or focus area identified in the previous chapter. To ensure that classroom observations are well received by teachers, I discuss ways of sharing the purpose of instructional innovation and the problem statement developed in Chapter 5 with them. This chapter provides guidelines for effective classroom observations, maintaining confidentiality in field notes, and focusing on instruction within a specified and short time frame. Additionally, I introduce how to unpack field notes using an observation inventory, which helps teaching teams gain insights into the instructional practices utilized by the teachers they observe. By following the strategies outlined in this chapter, instructional leaders and teaching teams can gather valuable information to address instructional challenges and ease the path to practical instructional innovation.

The Purpose and Benefits of Instructional Rounds

Instructional rounds can be implemented regularly by teaching teams to continuously observe and improve teaching and learning using an action research process to help guide their instructional innovation decisions (Tutt, 2022; Valenzuela, 2024a). Instructional rounds include strategically placing those responsible for instruction oversight directly in the classrooms they must impact. This structured protocol empowers teaching teams to enhance instruction utilizing three essential components: classroom observations, improvement plans, and a team approach to solving problems of practice (Meyer-Looze, 2015).

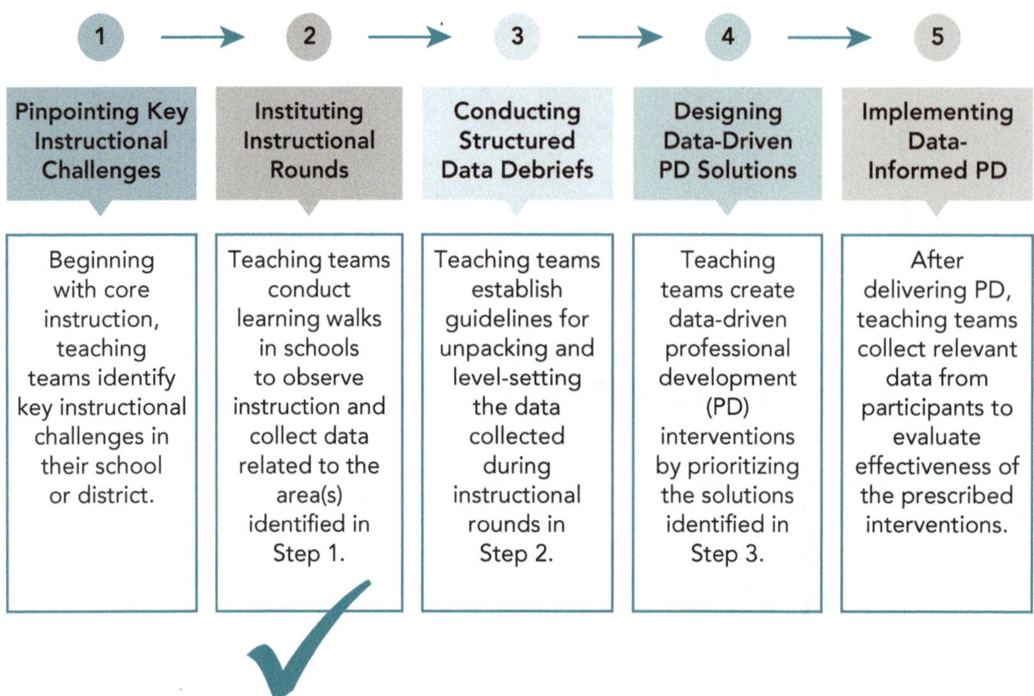

While the teaching team observes classrooms, they collect data and conduct a data debrief afterward to develop appropriate interventions. This inquiry-based process includes teachers exchanging timely feedback, finding solutions to problems of practice, and leveraging the collective wisdom in their schools (Hamilton et al., 2022).

In previous and recent years there has been growing interest in the impact of conducting instructional rounds. Here is a mix of some early and recent findings relevant to teaching teams:

- **Nurtured a collaborative culture:** Instructional rounds can foster a collaborative culture that supports learning (City et al., 2009).
- **Improved learning tasks:** The instructional rounds process provides a disciplined, collaborative way for schools and districts to focus on and improve specific learning tasks (City et al., 2009).
- **Improved teacher awareness:** A study found that instructional rounds improved educators' awareness about learner outcomes and effective teaching practices (Meyer-Looze, 2015).
- **Raised collective teacher efficacy:** School teaching teams that regularly observe one another's practices and see improved student outcomes through their collective efforts raise their collective efficacy (Wilson, 2020).
- **Improved teacher metacognition:** A study found that instructional rounds were an effective form of professional development (PD) that increased and matured teacher metacognition and self-efficacy (Hamilton et al., 2022).

Visiting classrooms will always be integral to designing effective and relevant development interventions in schools. Classrooms are the incubator for what is needed in a particular school, classroom, and education (Valenzuela, 2022g). It is challenging for anyone responsible for supervising and improving instruction to keep their fingers on the pulse of what is happening in their schools if they are not interacting with teachers in classrooms. Teachers are experts on their students and know their academic needs and often relevant aspects of their personal lives essential to know for motivating them (e.g., their interests, goals, and assets).

Listening to teachers is essential for instructional innovation. Classroom visits through instructional audits, instructional rounds, and learning walks are strategies teaching teams can leverage to collaborate with teachers to both learn from them and recommend appropriate tools and practices for empowering them.

Visiting Classrooms

While keeping the focus on instructional rounds, I'll quickly clarify the overlap and separate functions of learning walks, instructional rounds, and instructional audits for teaching teams and how they may be applied in their settings. I thought it vital to underscore well-known processes for conducting classroom visits and recognizing both their overlap and unique purposes. Although this chapter is focused on instructional rounds, some teaching teams may be considering conducting an instructional audit. I am making this distinction because audits employ similar processes to instructional rounds. These approaches are similar as they involve educators participating in classroom observations, discussions, and reflection to enhance teaching and learning. This is how they differ in their overall objectives:

1. Learning walks are brief classroom visits that educators can leverage to ascertain teaching and learning within their respective contexts (Short & Main, 2021). Learning walks are an integral component of the action research process and are therefore implemented during instructional audits and rounds to provide teaching teams with relevant data. Learning walks focus on teaching and learning and can even be conducted informally by teachers to help one another improve (Edutopia, 2018). For example, a beginning teacher may engage in a learning walk to observe and learn facilitation of differentiation strategies from a seasoned colleague.
2. Instructional rounds follow an inquiry process (City et al., 2009) and are integral for schools nurturing a culture of collaboration and continuous instructional innovation (Meyer-Looze, 2015; Principal's Playbook, n.d.). Although not evaluative, this process involves teaching teams conducting learning walks several times throughout the school year to observe teaching and learning, identify areas that need improvement, and collect the necessary

data for providing timely feedback (Meyer-Looze, 2015; Principal's Playbook, n.d.) and developing impactful PD. Instructional rounds involve a lengthy process that includes level-setting meetings, visiting classrooms, and data discussions but are more informal than instructional audits and can be conducted once a quarter or as needed. In the context of this book, teaching teams should comprise folks responsible for improving instruction in a school, such as assistant principals, lead teachers, instructional coaches, and teachers from various disciplines and content areas.

3. Instructional audits are used to identify the root causes of persistent student achievement and learning gaps existing within a space involving an extensive process that includes conducting learning walks, interviews, and focus groups (Institute for Research and Reform in Education, n.d.). Educators use what they glean to develop an understanding of how to coordinate the best curriculum-based instruction for producing high academic outcomes for learners (Albemarle County Public Schools, 2023; Hanover Research, 2023).

Now that we have gained a better understanding of the objectives and methods for visiting classrooms, we are ready to begin facilitating instructional rounds—moving us closer to carrying out instructional innovation through action research. It's worth noting that the learning walks your teaching team will embark on to visit classrooms are integral components of the greater instructional innovation system outlined in this section of the book. Your learning walks will therefore necessitate structure, purpose, and a thoughtful data debrief. The subsequent sections of this chapter provide concrete steps for seamlessly implementing these ideas throughout your instructional rounds.

Step-by-Step Guide for Conducting an Instructional Round

All of the collaborative practices and valuable advice in the preceding chapters of this book were purposefully provided to develop cohesive teaching teams knowledgeable enough to conduct fruitful instructional rounds. Leveraging your team's proper united understanding of core instruction and effective teamwork, this section serves as a guide, outlining the necessary steps to facilitate the instructional round process effectively.

Teaching teams should start instructional rounds referring to the problem statement they crafted (see Chapter 5) and use a structured learning walk process to gather pertinent data about their instructional innovation focus (see Figure 6.1). The rounds should be conducted every quarter of the school year to assess and plan the appropriate interventions for solving the instructional issues previously identified.

FIGURE 6.1: LEARNING WALK SCHEDULE

School District: ____________________

Learning Walks Date: ____________________

Team 1: ____________________ Team 3: ____________________

Team 2: ____________________

SCHOOL NAME				
10:00–10:15	Conference Room	Team 1	Team 2	Team 3
10:15–10:25		Rm: ___	Rm: ___	Rm: ___
10:30–10:40		Rm: ___	Rm: ___	Rm: ___
10:45–10:55		Rm: ___	Rm: ___	Rm: ___
11:00–11:10		Rm: ___	Rm: ___	Rm: ___
11:15	Conference Room	Debrief 11:15–11:45		

NOTE: Teaching teams can adapt this schedule as needed, including adjusting times, the number of teams, classroom visits, and debriefing timings to suit their unique needs better.

Through these 10 steps, teaching team leaders will find practical guidance for spearheading instructional innovation through action research in their schools (Valenzuela, 2024a).

Step 1: Teaching Team Leader Preparation

- Review the problem statement crafted by the teaching team (see Chapter 5) to ensure a clear focus.
- Understand the structured learning walk process (refer to the "Preparing for Instructional Learning Walks" section on page 95) and how it guides data collection during instructional rounds.
- Schedule quarterly instructional rounds to align with district and school assessment and intervention planning cycles.
- Create a schedule with timings and who will visit each of the classrooms.

Step 2: Team Briefing

- Conduct a preround briefing meeting with the entire teaching team.
- Review the problem statement and articulate the objectives of the instructional round to ensure each team member understands.
- Assign classroom visitation schedule, roles, and responsibilities to the teaching team members (e.g., classroom observers, data debrief note-takers).

Step 3: Observation Protocol for Learning Walk

- Review with the team a structured observation protocol closely aligned with the focus area specified in the problem statement.
- Provide the team members guidance on what to look for during the learning walk classroom visits (e.g., instructional strategies used, student engagement and motivation, curricular resources).
- Remind the team not to put the teacher's names on the protocol document and not to stay in the classroom longer than 10–15 minutes.

Step 4: Data Collection

- Conduct the learning walks by visiting classrooms in teams of 2–3 team members.
- It's OK to greet the teacher and the students when appropriate, ensuring not to disrupt teaching and learning.
- Adhere to the observation protocol and take notes on observations in the classroom.
- Encourage team members to document objectively and honestly.

Step 5: Debriefing Following Learning Walk

- Immediately following the learning walk, reconvene the teaching team to debrief.
- Facilitate shared observations using a structured protocol (see Figure 6.5).
- Discussions should not name specific teachers. Instead, they should focus on how students receive instruction and identifying common challenges across the observed classrooms.
- Ensure each team member sees and says the same things regarding the alignment between the problem statement and observed classroom practices.
- Conjure up solutions to the instructional problems observed.

Step 6: Analysis and Reflection

- Analyze the collected data to pinpoint the causes of the instructional challenges. If needed, revise the problem statement.
- Reflect on the implications of the findings to student learning and teacher pedagogical strategies.

- Specify the desired improvement outcomes.
- Consider potential PD interventions for producing the desired improvement outcomes.
- Documentation in this step doesn't have to be formal, but it will help inform the team's action plan. See Appendix A (page 172) for the action plan document.

Step 7: Action Planning

- See Appendix A (page 172) for the action plan document. The team's action plan is a project management tool for its instructional innovation endeavors.
- Collaboratively develop improvement plans to address the instructional issues identified.
- Define goals and outcomes, strategies, and timely implementation timelines.
- Assign the teaching team members duties and responsibilities for action planning and execution.

Step 8: Follow-Up and Monitoring

- Execute the developed action plan and make time for frequent monitoring.
- Meet with the teaching team regularly (preferably weekly) to review the effectiveness of the interventions. If the team determines a better course, feel free to make the necessary adjustments.
- During the teaching team meetings, continuously assess the impact of the interventions on student outcomes and teaching practice.

Step 9: Engage in Continuous Reflection and Iteration

- Examine and reflect on the outcomes of the instructional round and action research process.
- Identify key lessons and takeaways gleaned from the process.
- Identify key areas requiring further development.
- Plan subsequent iterations of the instructional rounds, refining problem statements, strategies, and outcomes as needed.

Step 10: Documentation and Sharing

- For each instructional round, assign a team member(s) to document findings, action plans, and outcomes throughout the entire process. Make this information accessible to the entire teaching team and district leaders. See Appendix A (page 172) for the action plan document.

- When appropriate, share insights and successes with other teaching teams within your school and school system.
- Use the documentation to inform level-setting and decision making as your teaching forges ahead toward continuous improvement.

By adapting and implementing these steps, teaching teams can conduct effective instructional rounds and engage in an action research process leading to an improved understanding of instructional innovation.

Expanding on Learning Walks and the Importance of Ongoing Classroom Visits

Although learning walks are defined at the beginning of this chapter, they are so crucial to the success of the instructional rounds process that we need to expand further on their significance in and implementation strategies in the subsequent sections of this chapter. Within the process of instructional rounds, the purpose of learning walks is to view instruction in real time and to reflect on practice (Edutopia, 2018). Learning walks should be held consistently—there shouldn't be surprises—let teachers know you're visiting their class; otherwise, trust and rapport could be broken with teachers.

However, learning walks can also be facilitated outside of the instructional rounds process. School leaders should conduct additional daily learning walks to keep abreast of the needs of their school, teaching staff, and students. Teaching team members should participate in learning walks with knowledge of the school's leadership and the consent of the teachers they visit. According to Jill Thompson and Crystal Xu (2021), there are four types of learning walks school leaders and teaching teams should participate in:

1. **Operational Learning Walks:** Focus on the school's facilities, schoolwide systems and practices, and critical classroom systems, vital operational aspects of a school day.
2. **Cultural Learning Walks:** Focus on what both teachers and students do. Teacher practice includes positive framing and tone during lessons. Student actions include engagement and participation.
3. **Instructional Learning Walks:** Focus on how students receive instruction and lesson facilitation practices to highlight trends in the effectiveness of utilizing instructional strategies. Instructional walks are conducted to ascertain the tempo and scale of instructional rounds within subjects and content-specific practices. Individual teachers can also conduct informal learning walks when looking to improve their facilitation of strategies. For this purpose, they seek out more experienced colleagues.

4. **Systems Learning Walks:** Focus on how time, resources, and the school faculty are utilized to maximize student benefits. Reviewing school enabling systems ensures they are correctly aligned with resources and school goals, clarified for all stakeholders, and strategically positioned to maximize impact.

For this chapter and for carrying out the instructional innovation process, I want you to focus on instructional learning walks during your instructional rounds.

Preparing for Instructional Learning Walks

Preparing a schedule for conducting learning walks to collect data as part of the instructional rounds process isn't difficult, but it's crucial to the success of the process. To streamline the preparation process, the team should focus on the following steps:

Step 1: Assign Roles. Decide which team members and teachers will be visiting classrooms and which teachers will be observed. You may also invite central office staff to participate in the process.

To earn the trust of the teaching staff, always remember to include one or two teachers who are on the teaching team in the learning walks and data debrief portions of the instructional rounds.

Step 2: Prepare a Learning Walk Protocol. When teaching team members visit classrooms, they need an instrument for making field notes. The learning walk protocol must align with the instructional focus of the learning walks and problem statement. See Figures 6.2, 6.3, and 6.4 for three adaptable versions of the learning walk protocol. Feel free to adapt and tweak this document per your teaching team's needs.

Step 3: Specify the Time Frame. Plan to spend 60 minutes visiting classrooms and 30 minutes on your data debrief. For example, learning walks will take place between 9:00 a.m. and 10:30 a.m.

Step 4: Create a Schedule. Assign two to three teaching team members to visit five teachers during the hour allotted for the learning walks. It's crucial not to stay longer than 10 minutes. See Figure 6.1 for a schedule template.

Step 5: Prepare a Debrief Protocol. Following the learning walks using a debriefing protocol will keep the team on track and schedule within 30 minutes (see Figure 6.5). Feel free to adjust the timings and the protocol to meet the needs of your teaching team.

Adhering to these steps in your preparation for instructional learning walks will enhance your team's efficiency and organization in the learning walk process. Additionally, these steps honor the collaborative and supportive team the teaching team developed in Chapter 1 of this book—which is crucial for sustained success.

FIGURE 6.2: LEARNING WALK PROTOCOL: DIFFERENTIATION

Note: Using ChatGPT, I defined the evidence criteria of the instructional focus of the learning walk (to the best of our ability, I edited this list to remove inaccurate material).

Focus: Differentiated instruction involves tailoring teaching methods to meet the diverse needs of students. There are various strategies for differentiation, and they can be broadly categorized into four main types:

1. **Content Differentiation:**
    - Adjusting the material being taught to suit the readiness level, interests, and learning profiles of individual students.
    - Providing alternative content or resources that cater to different learning styles or preferences.
    - Offering varied levels of complexity within the same topic to address diverse student abilities.
2. **Process Differentiation:**
    - Adapting the instructional methods and activities to accommodate different learning preferences and paces.
    - Incorporating a range of instructional strategies such as cooperative learning, project-based learning, or inquiry-based learning.
    - Allowing students to demonstrate understanding through different means, such as presentations, written reports, or multimedia projects.
3. **Product Differentiation:**
    - Allowing students to showcase their understanding of a concept through varied final products or assessments.
    - Offering a choice of projects that align with individual strengths or interests.
    - Encouraging creativity and independent thinking in the creation of final products.
4. **Learning Environment Differentiation:**
    - Modifying the physical or emotional learning environment to meet the needs of diverse learners.
    - Providing flexible seating arrangements to accommodate different learning preferences.
    - Creating a positive and supportive atmosphere that values diversity and encourages risk-taking.

FIGURE 6.3: LEARNING WALK PROTOCOL: ENGAGEMENT

Note: Using ChatGPT, I defined the evidence criteria of the instructional focus of the learning walk (to the best of our ability, I edited this list to remove inaccurate material).

Active Participation: Student engagement refers to the level of interest, motivation, and active participation that students exhibit in the learning process. It goes beyond completion of assignments; instead, it reflects the depth of a student's involvement, curiosity, and connection with the content. A highly engaged student is not just physically present but is mentally and emotionally invested in their learning experience.

1. **Active Learning Strategies:**
   - Students actively participate in group discussions, contributing ideas and collaborating with peers.
   - Students engage in problem-solving activities, applying theoretical concepts to real-world scenarios.
   - Students demonstrate practical application of knowledge by creating tangible outcomes, showcasing a deeper understanding of the subject.
2. **Technology Integration Strategies:**
   - Students enthusiastically interact with multimedia elements, such as videos and interactive presentations, enhancing their engagement with the material.
   - During online quizzes and polls, students actively participate, providing real-time responses and feedback.
   - Virtual field trips captivate students' attention, providing a dynamic and immersive learning experience.
3. **Inclusive Teaching Strategies:**
   - Diverse content and perspectives in the curriculum resonate with students, fostering a sense of connection and relevance.
   - Students explore topics through flexible learning paths, choosing options that align with their individual learning styles.
   - Active listening and feedback create an inclusive environment, where students feel valued and encouraged to share their thoughts.
4. **Assessment and Feedback Strategies:**
   - Formative assessments prompt students to demonstrate ongoing understanding, with adjustments made based on their responses.
   - Peer assessments involve students providing constructive feedback to their peers, promoting a collaborative learning atmosphere.
   - Reflection and self-assessment activities encourage students to evaluate their own progress, set goals, and take ownership of their learning journey.

FIGURE 6.4: LEARNING WALK PROTOCOL: LEARNING TARGETS AND TEACHING STRUCTURE

Note: Using ChatGPT, I defined the evidence criteria of the instructional focus of the learning walk (to the best of our ability, I edited this list to remove inaccurate material).

Learning targets and teaching structure implementation encapsulates effective teaching strategies as educators employ clear learning targets at the start of lessons, ensuring student understanding and connection to overarching goals. The teaching structure is seamlessly integrated, utilizing both direct instruction and flexible/individual grouping to cater to diverse learning needs and foster an engaging and differentiated learning environment.

1. **Learning Targets Implementation:**
    - Teachers clearly communicate learning targets at the beginning of the lesson, ensuring students understand the specific goals for the day.
    - Learning targets are prominently displayed in the classroom, providing a visual reference for students throughout the lesson.
    - Throughout the lesson, teachers refer back to the learning targets, connecting activities and discussions to the established goals.
2. **Teaching Structure—Direct Instruction:**
    - During the direct instruction phase, teachers present content clearly and concisely, providing explanations and examples to support understanding.
    - Teachers use a variety of instructional aids, such as visual aids, demonstrations, or multimedia, to enhance comprehension.
    - Students actively engage with the direct instruction, asking questions for clarification and participating in guided practice activities.
3. **Teaching Structure—Flexible and Individual Grouping:**
    - Teachers facilitate flexible grouping, allowing students to collaborate with peers based on their needs and preferences.
    - Individualized learning tasks are provided to cater to the diverse needs of students within each group.
    - Teachers circulate among groups, providing targeted support, feedback, and clarification as needed.
4. **Assessment and Feedback in Workshop Structure:**
    - Formative assessments are seamlessly integrated into the workshop structure, with teachers gauging student understanding through ongoing checks for understanding.
    - Teachers provide timely and specific feedback to individual students, addressing their strengths and areas for improvement.
    - Peer collaboration and feedback are encouraged during group activities, fostering a collaborative learning community.

The team lays the groundwork for meaningful classroom observations and impactful discussions that drive continuous instructional innovation in your school by focusing on role assignments, setting a schedule, and preparing your protocol documents. Don't worry if the entire process feels and appears clunky at first. Remember you'll conduct instructional rounds once per quarter, and the team will improve each time.

Learning Walk Protocol Reproducible(s)

The following learning walk protocol reproducible items are available for download and can be adapted by teaching teams to define their intended instructional focus. These documents are aligned with the core instruction themes addressed in this book.

Learning Walk Protocol

Learning Walk Focus: Differentiation of Instruction

Teacher: ______________________________

Date: ________________________________

Time: ________________________________

Grade/Content: _______________________

Remember that you are only observing and collecting evidence. Comments or feedback should be written without judgment.

I SAW (What the teacher and/or students are doing related to differentiation of instruction)

I HEARD (What the teacher and/or students are saying related to differentiation of instruction)

I WONDER (Thoughts about what you *didn't* see related to differentiation of instruction)

Specify differentiation strategies that best mirror the observed instruction. Refer to Figure 6.2 (page 96).

Content	Process	Product	Environment

Learning Walk Focus: Student Engagement

Teacher: ______________________________

Date: ______________________________

Time: ______________________________

Grade/Content: ______________________

Remember that you are only observing and collecting evidence. Comments or feedback should be written without judgment.

I SAW (What the teacher and/or students are doing related to student engagement)

I HEARD (What the teacher and/or students are saying related to student engagement)

I WONDER (Thoughts about what you *didn't* see related to student engagement)

Specify engagement strategies that best mirror the observed instruction. Refer to Figure 6.3 (page 97).

Active Learning	Technology Integration	Inclusive Teaching	Assessment and Feedback

Learning Walk Focus: Learning Targets and Workshop Structure

Teacher: ______________________

Date: ______________________

Time: ______________________

Grade/Content: ______________________

Remember that you are only observing and collecting evidence. Comments or feedback should be written without judgment.

I SAW (What the teacher and/or students are doing related to learning targets and teaching structure implementation)

I HEARD (What the teacher and/or students are saying related to learning targets and teaching structure implementation)

I WONDER (Thoughts about what you didn't see related to learning targets and teaching structure implementation)

Specify learning targets and workshop structure implementation strategies that best mirror the observed instruction. Refer to Figure 6.4 (page 98).

Learning Targets	Direct Instruction	Flexible and Individual Grouping	Assessment and Feedback

Student Learning Engagement and Participation

STUDENT ACTIONS	OBSERVED
Students answer questions with thoughtful analysis, synthesis, and well-reasoned responses.	☐ Yes ☐ No
Students effectively communicate their learning needs to the teacher.	☐ Yes ☐ No
Students expand their understanding by linking new ideas to what they've previously learned.	☐ Yes ☐ No
Students engage in academic discussions with peers.	☐ Yes ☐ No
Students collaborate with their peers, pooling ideas and working together to achieve shared learning goals.	☐ Yes ☐ No
Students seek mentorship from adults, benefiting from guidance and support to foster their educational and personal growth.	☐ Yes ☐ No
Students work independently.	☐ Yes ☐ No

Unpacking Field Notes From the Learning Walks and Leveraging Data for Continuous Improvement

We've established the importance of teaching teams implementing learning walks during quarterly instructional rounds as an integral component of the continuous action research process for achieving instructional innovation. However, following learning walks, it's critical to establish an effective methodology for gathering and processing the data gathered. This will ensure your team rounds and interventions are data driven, well informed from start to finish, and the means for facilitating informed decision making and targeted improvements in teaching practices.

Figure 6.5 is an adaptable protocol template teams can use to guide their data debriefs. A good rule of thumb is to have someone on the team record the team members' responses. The overall data should be consolidated and categorized to identify common themes. This process is straightforward and should be simple for any team to implement. However, getting it right is critical to the action research process and design of the PD interventions the team decides to implement. More of this process will be explained in Chapter 7 on pages 109–122.

FIGURE 6.5: LEARNING WALK DATA DEBRIEF PROTOCOL

LEARNING WALK DATA DEBRIEF PROTOCOL		
PROCESS	TIME	PERSON(S)
Glows: "I Saw . . ." Following the learning walk protocol, the teaching team begins the conversation by validating good teaching practice and sharing what they saw in alignment with the focus; everyone participates.	3 Minutes	Teaching Team
Grows: "I Saw . . ." The teaching team now shares the instructional areas that need improvement without mentioning teacher names; everyone participates.	3 Minutes	Teaching Team
Conjuring Up Solutions to Concerns: "Consider Using . . ." The teaching team shares ideas, strategies, and resources for improving teaching practice; the teaching staff listens and may respond; everyone participates.	4 Minutes	Teaching Team
Reflection and Open Conversation The teaching staff expresses what they gleaned from the data debrief and the steps they will take to refine practices collaboratively; everyone may engage in open conversation.	10 Minutes	Teaching Team
Total	**20 Minutes**	

Developed by Jorge Valenzuela of Lifelong Learning Defined, Inc.

Each line item of the protocol plays an important role in refining instructional practices. The data recorder should therefore categorize the teaching team responses into the following corresponding categories:

- **Glows:** Observed areas of strength
- **Grows:** Observed areas needing refinement
- **Concerns:** Areas lacking follow-through of performance expectations
- **Possible Solutions:** The team members suggest solutions (e.g., boost student engagement and improve literacy) and may also brainstorm possible interventions for improving the areas of growth.

By streamlining the organization of the teaching team responses into these categories, the action research process becomes more linear, actionable, and attainable—leading to continuous instructional innovation and refinement. Using this structured approach ensures the team's insights gleaned during the learning walks are effectively used to impact teaching and learning throughout the school, nurturing a collaborative culture of ongoing instructional innovation. Furthermore, analyzing data can be broken up into multiple work sessions to make these process steps less time-consuming following learning walks, as explained in more detail in Chapter 7 (page 141).

In this vignette, the principal ofThomas Hunter Middle School in Mathews County, Virginia, Laurel Byrd, describes how her teaching team's participation in an instructional round shifted her plans from training her teaching staff in project-based learning (PBL) to firming up their core instruction.

At the end of the first school year post-COVID-19, I contracted with Jorge to begin working on PBL at the middle school level, and his first suggestion was to conduct instructional rounds to make sure that the staff were ready for this initiative. I had never heard of learning walks or instructional rounds, but I loved intent and process! Just getting a snapshot of the state of core instruction is always a great idea! Since it was just myself and one assistant principal, Jorge also trained a group of teacher leaders. This was great for them as they were excited to get some experience in looking at instruction on a building level.

What we discovered was that our staff was not ready for schoolwide PBL! As we were emerging from COVID-19, our teachers needed to regroup and refocus on the basics while we addressed burnout, teachers' and students' mental health concerns, and widespread behavioral issues. Don't be afraid to say no to a new initiative when staff aren't ready! Take the time to really

(Continued)

(Continued)

get to know what is happening in your school! So rather than begin an initiative that was doomed to fail, Jorge was able to create PD based on solid core instruction that brought everyone back into focus. A few teachers complained that we were doing "the same old stuff"—but that's the stuff that works, so let's all do that! For new teachers, several of whom were career switchers, it was the instructional training that they needed to be successful. ●

In this vignette, Principal Byrd perfectly describes her teaching teams' first experience with learning walks during the instructional round just mentioned and the significant impact on their practice.

In order to conduct the learning walks, I chose a group of teacher leaders to help. First, Jorge trained us all in the simple procedures, and second, I emphasized to all staff that this was not a part of the evaluation process. This is important. We were simply looking for a "snapshot" of good core instruction. After a day of visiting classrooms, I met with the teacher leader group to debrief. First I asked, "What stood out to you from your data collection?" The group was able to look at data to find that our core instruction needed some shoring up. I then asked, "What did you learn from your visits?"

Wow. One teacher honestly said, "I suck. I saw this teacher using some great strategies that I know but have forgotten about in all that's going on. I was reminded what good teaching looks like, and I need to get back to it." While I disagree that this teacher "sucks," teachers need to see other teachers at work! All of the teachers in the group began to reflect on their own practice and what they took away personally. You can't get more powerful than that!

After that, I created days for every teacher in the building to do learning walks in other classrooms. Logistically, it can be tricky; however, anything worth doing is rarely easy! It rejuvenated them! They were reminded of strategies and connected with their colleagues! Thank-you emails started flying around, and collaboration was jump-started. After being isolated throughout the pandemic, teachers began to reach out to one another! ●

Chapter Summary

This chapter outlines three critical processes required for instructional innovation through action research. First, we dove into instructional rounds followed by learning walks for data collection and a protocol for streamlining the data debrief process. For each of these practices, I provided straightforward formats that teaching teams can readily adapt along with the necessary planning and implementation documents—a schedule, learning walk protocols for three distinct instructional focuses, and the data debrief protocol.

Implementing daily informal learning walks along with the structured formats laid out in this chapter frequently will provide your teaching team with the necessary chops for continued and sustainable action research. Now that we know how to collect data as part of the instructional rounds process, we are ready to learn how to unpack and glean critical insights from the data into a comprehensive action plan in Chapter 7.

Reflective Prompts for Individual Teaching Team Members

1. Reflect on your previous understanding of the instructional rounds process. Did the process in this chapter affirm or clarify the purpose and procedures for the instructional rounds process?
2. Consider your previous understanding and implementation of instructional learning walks. What excites you most about participating in them, and how are they integral to the overall instructional innovation process?
3. Imagine your teaching team debriefing a structured learning walk focusing on teaching differentiation. How would you facilitate the debrief protocol, ensuring each member feels their contributions are valued?

Reflective Prompts for Teaching Teams

1. Within the teaching team, discuss the instructional rounds process. How might the team begin assigning critical roles and duties for their first implementation?
2. Discuss the teaching team's most recent implementation of the instructional rounds. How did the teaching team leader(s) ensure that each member understood the purpose of their data collection? How did each member's insights from their data help collectively conjure interventions for future desired outcomes?
3. Why should quarterly instructional rounds be part of a continuous action research process? How can the teaching team ensure the teaching staff understands and embraces the process?

CHAPTER 7

Step 3: Analyzing Learning Walk Data and Identifying Solutions Through Structured Data Debrief

In this chapter, teaching teams learn and establish guidelines for discussing the data collected during the learning walks portion of their quarterly instructional rounds. They focus on identifying themes in their data, conjuring up possible solutions, and identifying barriers to addressing the instructional challenges they outlined in Step 1 and gleaned in Step 2. Through guided reflection using a discussion protocol, they consider both instructional strength and improvement to begin crafting a comprehensive action plan using a powerful template.

Teams also learn to do their best to align new teaching initiatives and existing practices, which is crucial for having teachers buy into instructional innovation efforts within their action plans. Guidelines for identifying potential barriers to success, such as strict pacing or heavy teacher workloads, and considering appropriate remedies are also discussed in this chapter.

Additionally, teaching teams are encouraged to consider solutions introduced in previous chapters of this book to improve core instruction, such as curriculum mapping and alignment, the use of community protocols, and research-informed ways of setting metrics for students' success. Furthermore, school teams establish a solid foundation for addressing instructional challenges and enhancing their teaching practices by engaging in needed discourse to explore the right solutions and interventions.

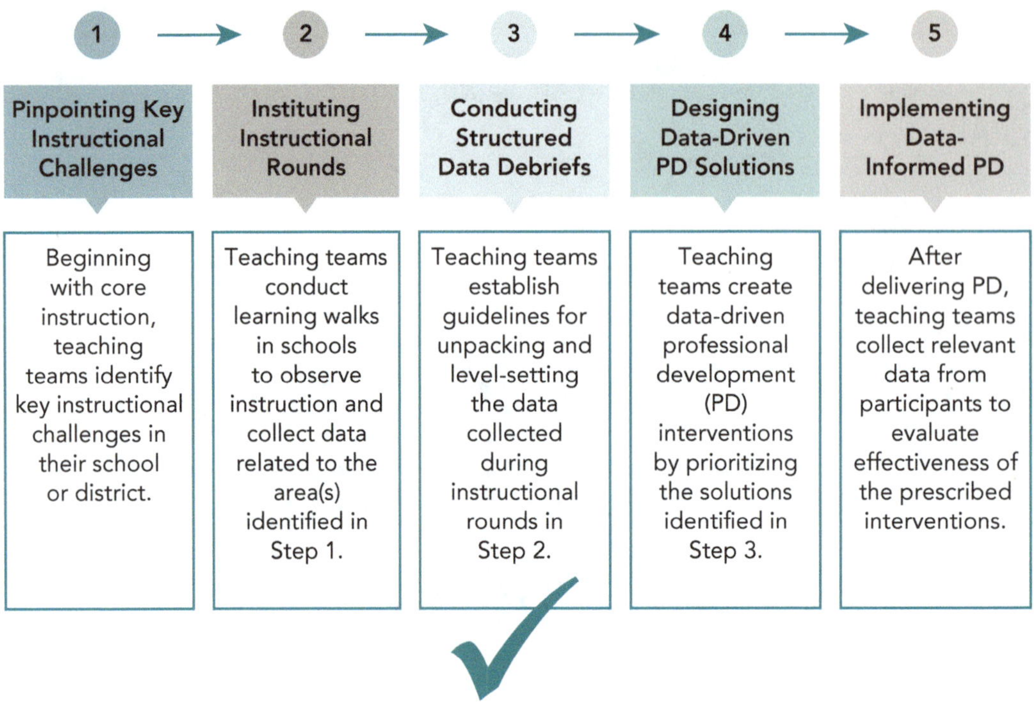

Significance of Action Plans in Instructional Innovation

Before your team learns to debrief learning walk data collections using a structured protocol, I want to discuss the significance of the development of action plans you'll encounter throughout this and the remaining chapters of this book. In Chapter 5 your team articulated the problem statement and the basis for your action research in the action plan document. Using the data from the instructional rounds and insights from the remaining chapters, the team will now focus on completing and revising the plans as needed.

Action plans are detailed blueprints and are part of project management, helping teams establish objectives, goals, outcomes, and timelines for tasks and solutions (Bridges, 2024). Moreover, action plans help teams set timelines for solutions as strategic tools teams use to prioritize tasks, track progress, and focus communication (Sambol, n.d.). There's more to come on timelines in Chapter 8 (page 123).

Some teams prefer virtual project management systems like Monday.com and Miro to create action plans supporting their workflow (Hartshorne, 2024; Miro, n.d.). I recommend getting started using the action plan document I made for you (see Appendix A on page 172 for the template). Familiarize your team with the action plan framework, and as your work evolves, you may want to use a system like Miro or Monday.com.

Data Discussion Protocols

Data are the backbone of action research, and teaching teams need reliable ways to examine data obtained during the learning walks portion of their instructional rounds. Educational data discussion protocols will be used to examine these data and address other critical items.

Moreover, data discussion protocols provide efficient and structured ways to have conversations and facilitate learning and problem solving for collaborative work (National School Reform Faculty, n.d.a). Protocols can be a facilitator's best friend, especially when they're trying to do something new and they don't want to miss critical steps. According to the National School Reform Faculty (n.d.a, n.d.b), some of the benefits of utilizing educational protocols by teaching teams may include the following:

- Provides a structure for analyzing and discussing data
- Fosters meaningful and efficient communication
- Demystifies new ideas and learning
- Provides the needed structure for collaborative problem solving
- Provides time and structure for active listening and reflection
- Ensures that all team voices are honored and heard
- Creates a safe space for providing timely and nonjudgmental feedback

Throughout the remaining chapters of this book, you'll find the steady practice of using various adaptable educational protocols and high-yielding strategies (Hattie, 2023). This is because I want teaching teams to have reliable and field-tested structures and procedures in place while they are carrying out the work.

Discussing and Analyzing Learning Walk Data Using a Structured Protocol

The Learning Walk Data Debrief Protocol (see Chapter 6, Figure 6.5, page 104) was developed to facilitate seamless discussion and disaggregation of the data gathered during learning walks. Categorizing findings is crucial to identifying common themes in the data—which are crucial to the following:

1. **Understanding Patterns and Trends:** The teaching team acts as researchers identifying recurring teams by gaining insight into patterns and trends in the data. For example, learning walks in multiple classrooms may uncover shared experiences across several classrooms—for instance, teachers not differentiating instruction effectively. Just as in the case of researchers, being able to recognize patterns and trends helps teaching teams understand underlying dynamics and informs their

decisions. Themes may also represent opinions (personal beliefs or judgments) and phenomena (observable events or occurrences in particular contexts or nature).

2. **Informing Interventions:** The teaching team becomes aware of instructional areas that need refining when themes are common in multiple classroom settings. For example, suppose the team notices the emerging theme of low student engagement in multiple classroom visits during learning walks. In that case, they can design targeted interventions to improve the teachers' use of engagement strategies.

3. **Guiding Next Steps:** Themes found in the data guide action steps toward improvement. After teaching teams identify the issue(s), they can work together to conjure up specific interventions and strategies. For example, if a theme revolves around waning interest in a mathematics or English language arts unit, action steps may involve helping students make real-world connections to the new concepts along with relatable examples and expert modeling.

   Note: The interventions identified by the team in this step do not have to be set in stone and will be fully explored in the next section. While designing interventions, teaching teams must identify barriers to success. During that reflection process, they may realize that the intervention they previously considered may not be the best course of action.

4. **Teaching Team and Stakeholder Engagement:** The themes identified by teaching teams provide both them and their stakeholders (teachers, students, and the community) with a shared perspective and common language around instructional issues. Collaboration can, therefore, become more effective because the collective sees and says the same things.

5. **Avoiding Biases and Assumptions:** Perceptions can play a significant role in allowing bias and assumptions to impact the teaching team's decisions. The systematic thematic analysis of data ensures a more objective comprehension of the existing instructional problems. This is crucial for ensuring your teaching team's action research is valid and reliable.

Using these guidelines to identify common themes in the data will empower teaching teams to make inferences and data-driven decisions, implement targeted interventions, and nurture instructional innovation in schools. Remember this process is ongoing. The following vignette illustrates the process of analyzing data obtained through learning walks to identify themes, design targeted interventions, and roll them out collaboratively and in phases.

The teaching team at King High School used the Learning Walk Data Debrief Protocol following a series of learning walks to observe classroom instruction systematically. Upon reviewing the data obtained from these walks, they noticed several teachers across various subjects exhibited similar instructional challenges. For instance, the collected data showed ineffective differentiation strategies in both English and mathematics classes. The team categorized the findings into common themes, such as "low engagement" and "lack of differentiation." Identifying these patterns allowed the team to recognize that the underlying issue affected multiple classrooms and wasn't isolated. Analyzing the data showed that these patterns represented both observable events and teacher practices, revealing a broader issue of students not responding to learning experiences.

The team devised targeted professional development (PD) interventions focused on differentiated instruction and engagement strategies to build on the identified themes. The PD was implemented in phases and tailored to address the specific needs observed across the classrooms. Initial workshops were tried, facilitated, and refined with a few teachers before broader application to other classrooms. Doing so ensured that interventions were adjusted based on feedback and effectiveness. Additionally, the teaching team fostered a shared understanding of the instructional issues and interventions by engaging with stakeholders, including teachers, students, and select community members. This structured approach enhanced the team's ability to collaborate and use data-driven decision making to support continuous instructional innovation at their school. ●

Note: The following section, "Identifying Solutions and Barriers to Success and Creating Alignment to Existing Priorities," is a separate session from the work carried out in the section "Discussing and Analyzing Learning Walk Data Using a Structured Protocol." Teaching teams may wish to discuss barriers and solutions immediately following their initial data debrief, and that's fine. However, since learning walks were conducted before the data debrief, doing it all in one day may be time-consuming. I recommend scheduling a meeting shortly after the initial data debrief to maintain the team's momentum to ensure timely action planning. Be sure to allocate ample time to allow for thorough discussion and brainstorming without rushing.

Identifying Solutions and Barriers to Success and Creating Alignment to Existing Priorities

Your teaching team has completed learning walks, analyzed the collected data, pinpointed themes in the data, and even listed possible solutions to the instructional problems identified. Now, what do you do with this information? It is necessary to structure this section as both a framework and a systematic approach to guide teaching teams as they address solving the instructional problems they identified through their data analysis. Identifying interventions and the barriers to success, and creating alignment to existing priorities, is critical to designing the right solutions for your school and fully engaging as researchers in action research. Putting this information into the action plan document provides logical flow of the process. See Appendix A (page 172) for the action plan document.

The first time your team works through this process may be unfamiliar and tedious—especially when completing the action plan document. That's OK and part of the course. Work through the process and understand what needs to be done to analyze the data to be able to conjure up solutions thoughtfully and carefully. Because action research for school transformation is ongoing, your team will improve through engaging in this process multiple times. Encourage collaboration by emphasizing the importance of each team member contributing their ideas and perspectives. This will create a sense of ownership and buy-in for the solutions put forward by the teaching team.

Here's the framework for learning how your teaching team can collaboratively analyze data and document solutions in your action plan effectively.

Step 1: Craft the Problem Statement

- **Craft the problem statement.** The problem statement could have been written before the team's initial formal instructional round (see Chapter 5). The problem statement sets the stage for successful action research and guides the teaching team toward data-informed solutions tailored to their specific teaching context. I recommend teaching teams co-create and revise actionable and realistic problem statements. Problem statements should initially identify the team's current situation regarding a particular instructional problem(s), briefly describe what needs to be improved, and articulate the desired outcomes to achieve the goal(s). Problem statements can be revised at any time during the action research process.
- **Consider the components of improvement and desired outcomes.** For teaching teams to have clarity about pinpointing precisely what they're looking to improve as articulated by the problem statement, I recommend drilling down what components of instruction require improvement. Additionally, I suggest identifying the desired outcomes of making that improvement.

See Figure 7.1 for a completed example of this section of the action plan document (also available in Appendix A, page 176).

Step 2: Analyze Learning Walk Data to Identify Instructional Issues

- **Review themes for instructional problems.** Quickly revisit the themes and patterns of the instructional challenges previously identified during the initial data debrief following learning walks (student engagement, classroom

FIGURE 7.1: COMPLETED EXAMPLE OF THE "CRAFT THE PROBLEM STATEMENT" (STEP 1) SECTION OF THE ACTION PLAN DOCUMENT

Step 1:

Craft the Problem Statement

A good problem statement sets the stage for successful action research and guides the teaching team toward data-informed solutions tailored to their specific teaching context. We recommend teaching teams co-create and revise actionable and realistic problem statements. Problem statements should initially identify the team's current situation regarding a specific instructional problem(s), briefly describe what needs to be improved, and articulate the desired outcomes to achieve the goal(s). Problem statements can be revised at any time during the course of the action research process.

- *At Walker Elementary observable issues include poor teacher morale, limited student engagement and participation, and consistently low reading scores among third-grade students.*

Components of Improvement and Desired Outcomes

- ***Teacher morale and attitudes toward their work***
  - *Increased job satisfaction among teaching staff*
  - *Improved morale and enthusiasm in daily teaching activities*
  - *Higher retention rates of experienced teachers*
- ***Student engagement and participation in daily lessons***
  - *Increased active participation in classroom discussions and activities*
  - *Improved student interest in daily learning goals*
  - *Enhanced collaboration among students*
- ***Reading comprehension and proficiency levels among third-grade students***
  - *Higher average scores on reading comprehension assessments*
  - *Increased number of students reading at or above grade level*
  - *Improved fluency and comprehension in reading tasks*

management, lack of differentiation, etc.) as a refresher. Categorize by aligning them to student outcomes or any other metric your school uses (e.g., priority standards). I suggest keeping student achievement, engagement, motivation, and attendance at the forefront of your intended outcomes.

Considering metrics other than the data obtained in the learning walks is also acceptable in this step. In this context, metrics may include data points such as student performance data, curriculum alignment, teacher self-assessment data, inclusivity practices, or any other critical data points.

- **Brainstorm interventions.** Have a note-taker jot down possible interventions to the identified instructional problems (instructional alignment, differentiation, etc.). Don't overthink this by overexplaining each intervention identified on paper. However, you may allow time for an explanation of the listed interventions for team members to learn about how they're used to address instructional problems for the first time.

- **Incorporate research-informed strategies.** Be sure that your team's interventions incorporate research-informed strategies and are grounded in evidence-based practice. Be honest about who on the teaching team or in the organization is qualified to successfully carry out the intervention through PD. The team may also have to brainstorm a reputable PD provider to coach them on new skills and strategies. Getting this right is very important. Botched PD lessens the trust of the teaching staff.
- **Prioritize interventions.** Discuss and rank the priority level for each intervention based on their impact on student outcomes and implementation feasibility based on the time required to carry out effectively. Also, identify who on the teaching staff and teaching team needs to participate in the PD. Do not have your folks attend PD they don't need. Remember that the targeted use of time, resources, and personnel helps earn and maintain trust.

See Figure 7.2 for a completed example of this section of the action plan document (also available in Appendix A, page 177).

FIGURE 7.2: COMPLETED EXAMPLE OF THE "ANALYZE LEARNING WALK DATA TO IDENTIFY INSTRUCTIONAL ISSUES" (STEP 2) SECTION OF THE ACTION PLAN DOCUMENT

Step 2:

Analyze Learning Walk Data to Identify Instructional Issues

Revisit previously identified instructional challenges from learning walks, categorizing themes by aligning them with student outcomes or other relevant metrics (e.g., priority standards). Consider additional data points beyond learning walks, such as student performance, curriculum alignment, teacher self-assessment, and inclusivity practices, to inform the review process.

- ***Poor teacher morale***
- ***Limited student engagement and participation***
- ***Low reading scores for third grade***

Brainstorm Interventions

Identify possible interventions to the identified instructional problems (instructional alignment, differentiation, etc.).

- ***Poor teacher morale:*** *Stress management and work–life balance training*
- ***Limited student engagement:*** *Engagement strategies workshop for elementary students*
- ***Low reading scores for third grade:*** *Foundational Literacy Workshop: Enhancing Reading Instruction for Third Grade*

Prioritize Interventions

Discuss and rank the priority level for each intervention based on their impact on student outcomes and implementation feasibility. Also, identify who on the teaching staff and teaching team needs to participate in the PD.

- ***Poor teacher morale:*** *Stress management and work–life balance training, Level 1 (5 teachers)*
- ***Limited student engagement:*** *Engagement strategies workshop for elementary students, Level 1 (3 teachers)*
- ***Low reading scores for third grade:*** *Foundational Literacy Workshop: Enhancing Reading Instruction for Third Grade, Level 1 (entire third-grade reading team)*

Highlight Positive Outcomes

Articulate the positive outcomes you hope to achieve from the successful implementation of the interventions; everyone participates.

Step 3: Identify Potential Barriers

- **Identify potential barriers.** Barriers to success prevent solutions to the identified instructional problems. The teaching team should now note the barriers they anticipate hindering the successful implementation of the prescribed interventions in classrooms. Common barriers may include resistance to change, competing district initiatives, time constraints, restrictive pacing, and limited resources.
- **Identify strategies for overcoming barriers.** Collectively offer practical strategies for overcoming the identified barriers. Strategies for overcoming the barriers listed in the previous bullet can include holding individual discussions with resisters, creating alignment between district initiatives, collaborating with stakeholders, freeing teachers up more, easing pacing guidelines, and improving resource allocation.

See Figure 7.3 for a completed example of this section of the action plan document (also available in Appendix A, page 177).

FIGURE 7.3: COMPLETED EXAMPLE OF THE "IDENTIFY POTENTIAL BARRIERS" (STEP 3) SECTION OF THE ACTION PLAN DOCUMENT

Step 3:

Identify Potential Barriers

Identify anticipated barriers that may impede successful implementation of interventions in classrooms. Consider potential obstacles such as resistance to change, competing district initiatives, time constraints, restrictive pacing, and limited resources.

- ***Poor teacher morale:*** *Resistant staff members*
- ***Limited student engagement:*** *Strict pacing*
- ***Low reading scores:*** *Time constraints*

(Continued)

(Continued)

Strategies for Overcoming Barriers

Collectively offer practical strategies for overcoming the identified barriers.

- ***Poor teacher morale:*** *Collaborative professional development and mentorship program*
- ***Limited student engagement:*** *Flexible pacing strategies, interactive and hands-on activities, and incorporation of technology and multimedia*
- ***Low reading scores:*** *Integrated reading activities, extended learning opportunities, and use of technology and digital tools*

Step 4: Develop Action Plans

- **Formulate action steps.** Collaborate with the team to develop actionable steps for implementing solutions.
- **Encourage setting SMART goals.** Setting SMART (specific, measurable, achievable, relevant, and time-bound) goals is a respected framework used by organizations (Leapsome Team, n.d.). Use it to assist the team with ensuring clarity in both goal attainment and accountability in action plans.
- **Assign responsibilities.** Clearly define the roles for effectively executing action plans for each member of the teaching team.
- **Monitor and evaluate.** Discuss and settle on metrics and long-term monitoring methods for evaluating the progress and effectiveness of the implemented solutions.
- **Create alignment with current overlapping initiatives.** In spaces where teaching teams are required to implement a district- or state-mandated instructional initiative (a reading program, project-based learning [PBL], standards-based assessments, etc.), reflect collectively and create necessary alignment. This is critical for teacher and stakeholder buy-in.

See Figure 7.4 for a completed example of this section of the action plan document (also available in Appendix A, page 178).

FIGURE 7.4: COMPLETED EXAMPLE OF THE "DEVELOP ACTION PLANS" (STEP 4) SECTION OF THE ACTION PLAN DOCUMENT

Step 4:

Develop Action Plans

When refining action plans, prioritize addressing underlying problems and enhancing student success. Effective PD interventions equip educators with transformative tools for teaching and learning. Implementing well-developed solutions enhances instructional practices and improves student learning outcomes. Teaching teams may have to seek assistance from an outside thought partner or consultant to develop logical, coherent, and sustainable action plans.

ISSUE	SOLUTIONS	POSSIBLE PD INTERVENTIONS
Poor Teacher Morale	1. Provide struggling teachers with a support partner. 2. Create opportunities for collaborative planning. 3. Establish regular opportunities for check-ins and feedback.	1. Stress management and work–life balance training 2. Positive reinforcement and feedback strategies workshops 3. Effective communication and conflict resolution workshops.
Limited Student Engagement	1. Introduce classroom projects aimed at having students explore their interests and passions. 2. Implement differentiated instruction to personalize learning for students with diverse interests and academic needs. 3. Create a positive and inclusive classroom culture that nurtures participation and peer collaboration.	1. PBL and effective use of technology tools to support learning workshops 2. Training in strategies for building rapport with students 3. Workshops on student-centered teaching strategies
Low Reading Scores	1. Implement a tiered literacy program focusing on phonics, vocabulary, and reading comprehension. 2. Provide targeted tiered interventions for struggling readers. 3. Create a culture that supports reading through book clubs and reading challenges.	1. Science of reading workshops 2. Assessing student reading levels training 3. Strategies for integrating literacy across the curriculum to promote reading fluency workshops

Ensure Continuous Improvement

- **Reflect and iterate.** Impress upon the team the importance of ongoing reflection and iteration in the instructional innovation process—including elements within this framework.
- **Adapt solutions.** Remain flexible and open to feedback, as well as pushback, by adjusting solutions based on current themes and trends discovered in observations.
- **Celebrate successes.** It's healthy and desired to take time to acknowledge and celebrate team wins as doing so can boost the team's motivation and momentum.

In closing, the process outlined in this framework is not a one-and-done solution to instructional innovation in your school. Instead, it's an ongoing commitment teaching teams can use to adapt, tweak, and take ownership of the process for continuous refinement and innovation. It is one of the ways your action research comes to life within the pages of a personalized action plan. Moreover, the steps outlined and the action plan worksheet (see Figures 7.1, 7.2, 7.3, and 7.4) provide the necessary guidance for teams to effectively analyze data, conjure solutions, and synergize enhanced student outcomes.

Always be mindful of carrying out your interventions with adapted research-informed strategies, putting the right personnel in place, and addressing the barriers to success. Ensure clarity in your action plans by using SMART goals (Leapsome Team, n.d.) and thoughtfully assigning tasks and responsibilities among the team. Align and monitor progress with school system priorities and foster cohesion and team consensus. Lastly, embrace reflection and flexibility and celebrate team wins along the way. Dedication to this process can help your teaching team create a culture of excellence in instructional innovation.

Instructional Rounds in Practice

The following vignette shares insights into working through the instructional rounds process by contributor Sara Leone and her colleagues at Summit Public Schools in Chicago, Illinois.

Instructional rounds have proven to be an effective practice in improving teaching and learning outcomes in our district. When our district committed to the instructional rounds process, administrators and teachers shared a unique opportunity to collaborate around instruction. By observing and discussing classroom instruction together, we gained valuable insights into effective teaching practices, identified areas for improvement, and shared innovative strategies. This collaborative approach fostered a culture of continuous improvement and supported the professional growth of educators and reestablished principals as instructional leaders of their schools.

By implementing instructional rounds districtwide, we noticed an increase in collaboration and a strengthening of the school's culture. Throughout the process, collaborative teams visited classrooms and experienced firsthand diverse instructional practices, which inspired the use of innovative strategies in others, supported collaboration focused on instructional practice and student outcomes, and identified areas for meaningful targeted PD. As a result of this process, as a district, we began to view instruction differently. In many ways, the instructional rounds propelled us toward responsive professional development rooted in what we identified were needs in our classrooms, not what was trending in education. Once committed to the process, it has become part of our district identity, and has allowed us to seamlessly respond to what is happening in classrooms to strengthen instruction and propel us to the next level. ●

Chapter Summary

In this chapter, teaching teams took their action research to the next level by learning to organize and create action plans by comprehensively approaching data analysis and solution development. The importance of leveraging learning walk data, educational protocols, and frameworks was highlighted and modeled throughout this chapter's content. Implementing interventions with research-informed strategies was also prioritized for teaching teams' consideration.

Additionally, teaching teams were reminded of their crucial roles and responsibilities within the team. Not leaving victory to chance, they were encouraged to identify solutions to success barriers, ensuring a well-thought-out implementation of interventions. Defining SMART goals, roles and responsibilities within the team, and metrics for long-term monitoring were underscored as paramount for developing collaborative plans. Furthermore, the significance of aligning instructional innovation to existing efforts to maximize resources and garner stakeholder support was emphasized within action plans, further highlighting the importance of sustainability in this process.

Moreover, this chapter provides a clear guide for teaching teams to engage in data-driven collaborative level-setting, problem solving, and decision making to drive instructional innovation and action research in schools. These steps and information seamlessly segue into Chapter 8, which provides further guidance for creating professional development interventions that prioritize solutions and positive student learning outcomes.

Reflective Prompts for Individual Teaching Team Members

1. Reflect on your previous experience in data analysis, solution development, and action planning. Did the process outlined throughout this chapter clarify and evolve your understanding of the significance of having a linear process? What are your specific takeaways?
2. Reflect on your role within the teaching team. How did the emphasis on roles and responsibilities impact your view on the collaborative teamwork necessary for instructional innovation?
3. What are the barriers to success at your current school? What are the strategies that you envision can help overcome them, and how would you convey that effectively to the teaching team?

Reflective Prompts for Teaching Teams

1. How did the dynamics within your teaching team evolve during the implementation of the various elements of action planning? What areas of collaborative teams need addressing and further development?
2. Reflect on the action plans developed following the guidance in this chapter. What tweaks are necessary to maximize outcomes and long-term sustainability? Why is instructional innovation through action research continuous and ongoing?
3. Reflect on the advice to align existing best practices and the needs of stakeholders with the team's action plan. How effectively is your team creating and demonstrating this alignment? What steps can your team take to enhance alignment and garner increased stakeholder buy-in?

CHAPTER 8

Step 4: Designing Data-Driven Professional Development Interventions for Solutions

In this chapter, teaching teams dedicate time to refining their action plan(s) by creating data-driven professional development (PD) interventions prioritizing solutions identified in Step 3. They begin to understand the importance of designing personalized and integrated PD solutions that are categorized into strands and milestones. Steps for developing PD strands cater to administrators, beginning teachers, and experienced teachers differently by ensuring their unique needs are highlighted. Teams also learn the significance and methodology of establishing a timeline with milestones to address solutions systematically.

Additionally, teaching teams are encouraged to cultivate internal talent to facilitate PD solutions to ensure long-term retention and growth and seek assistance from external collaborators to support their development in some instances. By designing data-driven PD solutions that are specific to their teaching staff and setting a clear timeline, the team lays the foundation for effective professional growth, as outlined in these pages.

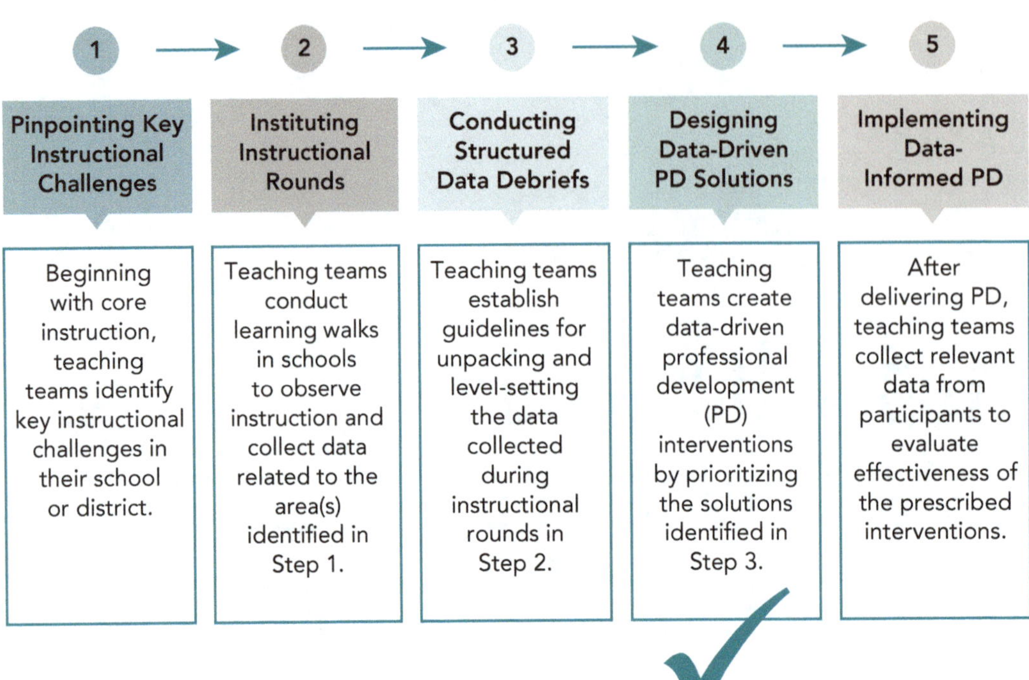

Utilizing Multiple Metrics for Tailored Professional Development

In action research, designing data-driven PD interventions and solutions to pursue effective pedagogical practices is essential (Clark et al., 2020). This process enables teaching teams to make evidence-based decisions and tailor PD to the needs of students, teachers, and the school community. It also provides a system for identifying learning gaps, tracking progress, and adapting instructional strategies from an informed perspective (Innovare, 2024). Sometimes, educators try new strategies and collect data to assess their impact on student learning. It's acceptable to not work in isolation and consider these and other pertinent metrics in this part of the action plan development process.

Action research is always situational and context based (Clark et al., 2020), so it is crucial for teams to broaden their perspective beyond the data obtained in learning walks from instructional rounds. As an author, I don't want to select metrics for your teaching team—I just want you to know it's all right to align efforts and other data collections critical to your school. By incorporating additional metrics, such as student performance data and student attendance (among other items) in action plans, you can create a more comprehensive framework for identifying PD interventions and solutions to instructional problems, thereby addressing a wider range of needs.

Guiding Principles for Effective Professional Development Interventions: Finding Solutions

PD interventions for educators in a specific school should not be one-size-fits-all; they must integrate various solutions to accommodate all teaching staff. They should be developed from a data-driven approach articulated in an action plan (see Chapter 7) (Hirsch et al., 2018). The distinction between a PD intervention and a solution resides in their separate yet connected roles within the teaching team's action plan. PD interventions are not the remedy to instructional problems—they serve as a tool to support the implementation of the solution (Darling-Hammond et al., 2017).

Note: Although PD interventions aim to support the implementation of solutions articulated in a school's action plan, it's essential to recognize that issues plaguing performance, such as low teacher morale, can significantly negatively impact instruction. Although traditionally it wasn't viewed as an instructional issue, it can and should be addressed in the team's action plans.

PD interventions involve educators participating in specialized workshops, programs, and activities to enhance their knowledge, skills, and instructional pedagogical practices (Darling-Hammond et al., 2017). Although interventions provide them with the skills needed to address instructional issues, they alone are not a panacea for underlying problems. Conversely, solutions to instructional issues encompass a comprehensive rectification approach (Monardo, 2017). Comprehensive solutions in education may include varied approaches—such as adapting new instructional strategies, improving school culture and climate, revamping curricula, introducing or improving educational policy, creating new assessments, improving classroom management, or revising pacing.

When refining action plans, teaching teams should focus on how their proposed solutions address the underlying causes of problems and aim to improve students' success. If your team feels unsure of what to do when faced with different issues from our examples and needs to come up with your own solutions and interventions, I recommend enlisting a thought partner. Preferably, this should be someone who has already overcome a similar instructional issue and implemented interventions. Lastly, effective PD interventions give educators the tools to transform teaching and learning, and implementing well-developed solutions improves instructional practices and student learning outcomes. See Table 8.1 for three common issues that negatively impact positive student outcomes and examples of how teaching teams can effectively address solutions and interventions within their action plans.

Devising action plans may be overwhelming for teaching teams, depending on the number of issues, solutions, and interventions identified (see Table 8.1). This is why building cohesive and collaborative teams is integral to the action research process (see Chapter 1). Before diving into the interventions, consider your school's culture and the team's level of trust with the teaching staff. In a profession already facing chronic shortages and teacher burnout (Bryant et al., 2023), reconciling solutions also involves strategically creating PD strategies and milestone timelines, as you will glean in the subsequent sections of this chapter.

TABLE 8.1: STRATEGIES AND PROFESSIONAL DEVELOPMENT INTERVENTIONS FOR ADDRESSING EDUCATIONAL CHALLENGES

ISSUE	SOLUTIONS	PD INTERVENTIONS
Poor Teacher Morale	1. Provide struggling teachers with a support partner. 2. Create opportunities for collaborative planning. 3. Establish regular opportunities for check-ins and feedback.	1. Stress management and work–life balance training 2. Positive reinforcement and feedback strategies workshops 3. Effective communication and conflict resolution workshops
Limited Student Engagement	1. Introduce classroom projects aimed at having students explore their interests and passions. 2. Implement differentiated instruction to personalize learning for students with diverse interests and academic needs. 3. Create a positive and inclusive classroom culture that nurtures participation and peer collaboration.	1. Project-based learning and effective use of technology tools to support learning workshops 2. Training in strategies for building rapport with students 3. Workshops on student-centered teaching strategies
Low Reading Scores	1. Implement a tiered literacy program focusing on phonics, vocabulary, and reading comprehension. 2. Provide targeted tiered interventions for struggling readers. 3. Create a culture that supports reading through book clubs and reading challenges.	1. Science of reading workshops 2. Assessing student reading levels training 3. Strategies for integrating literacy across the curriculum to promote reading fluency workshops

Developing Targeted Professional Development Strands

Too often, PD is one-size-fits-all and will not adequately improve outcomes for learners (Bondie et al., 2019), strengthen practice and morale, and build a positive culture of practice within the staff. Knowing and categorizing the actual needs of everyone empowers teaching teams to maximize the best use of common planning time, teaching team meetings, and districtwide in-service days. In this section of the action plan (see Table 8.2 and Appendix A, page 178), the team reconciles the solutions from Step 3 (see Chapter 7) to develop data-driven PD solutions (Hirsch et al., 2018). This includes articulating targeted, tailored, and embedded PD solutions in strands and milestones to ensure that every component of the action plan is strategically designed to meet educators' needs and align with the overall objectives of the action plan.

TABLE 8.2: TARGETED PROFESSIONAL DEVELOPMENT INTERVENTION STRANDS

ISSUE	ADMINISTRATOR STRAND	BEGINNING TEACHER STRAND	SEASONED TEACHER STRAND
Poor Teacher Morale	1. Morale-Boosting Strategies Workshop 2. Cultivating a Positive School Culture Training 3. Empathetic Leadership and Support Seminar	1. Classroom Management Essentials Workshop 2. Differentiated Instruction Techniques Training 3. Building Rapport With Students Seminar	1. Renewing Passion in Teaching Retreat 2. Advanced Strategies for Teacher Well-Being Workshop 3. Cultivating Resilience in Experienced Educators Seminar
Limited Student Engagement	1. Understanding Factors That Promote Student Engagement Workshop 2. Engagement Strategies Across the Curriculum Workshop	1. Understanding Factors That Promote Student Engagement Workshop 2. Engagement Strategies Across the Curriculum Workshop	1. Advanced Strategies for Student Engagement Workshop 2. Incorporating Technology for Enhanced Student Engagement Training
Low Reading Scores	1. Comprehensive Literacy Intervention Workshop 2. Targeted Reading Strategies Seminar 3. Fostering a Reading Culture Training	1. Foundational Literacy Instruction Workshop 2. Strategies for Supporting Struggling Readers Seminar 3. Cultivating a Reading Community Session	1. Advanced Literacy Strategies for Seasoned Teachers 2. Tailored Interventions for Diverse Learners Workshop 3. Fostering a Reading Culture in Experienced Classrooms Workshop

To effectively address the needs of diverse teaching staff, strands for tiered curriculum design and facilitation strategies should support administrators, beginning teachers, and seasoned teachers differently (Valenzuela, 2022j), even as it pertains to the same topic (see Table 8.2). Teaching teams getting this right for the instructional staff is super important.

1. **Strands for Administrators:** In this context, the administrator's role is to nurture and foster a supportive environment conducive to teacher growth and development. PD strands for administrators should focus on best supporting teachers' implementations with students (see Table 8.2). Other PD strands for administrators may include leadership skills, culture-building strategies, and instructional coaching techniques. If administrators are not built up to develop into instructional leaders, many will become low-level managers at best. I say

low-level because they will not be able to support the instructional needs of the teachers they supervise adequately.

2. **Strands for Beginning Teachers:** Beginning teachers (BTs) need a solid foundation in core instruction and instructional alignment (see Chapters 3 and 4). Additionally, many need targeted PD interventions in rapport and relationship building with students, classroom management, lesson planning, and implementation of instructional strategies (facilitating flexible grouping, direct instruction, etc.). Strands for BTs should build foundational knowledge and be practical (see Table 8.2).

3. **Strands for Seasoned Teachers:** Seasoned teachers have vast knowledge and experience, and their PD time should be honored and well spent. They are exemplary performers (see Chapter 2 on page 36) and benefit most from PD strands that deepen their pedagogical knowledge, expose them to new innovative teaching strategies, and engage them in reflection on their current practice. For seasoned and experienced teachers, PD can include overview refreshers as needed, advanced topics, specific content, peer mentoring, and leadership development.

To build trust with teachers, I cannot stress the significance of the team taking the time to make these distinctions between the PD strands. Also, if applicable to their roles, be sure to include elective teachers and those on teacher contracts (such as counselors). This is a practice I highly recommend in all schools looking to nurture a culture of continuous growth in their staff by meeting them where they are. Finally, a timeline with milestones should be set for tackling the solutions logically and coherently (see the following Tables 8.3, 8.4, and 8.5 as well as Appendix A, pages 180–182).

TABLE 8.3: EXAMPLE 1: TIMELINE AND MILESTONES FOR PROFESSIONAL DEVELOPMENT INTERVENTION

ISSUE	SEMESTER	MILESTONES, PD STRANDS, AND INTERVENTIONS
Poor Teacher Morale	**Summer**	1. **Administrators:** Morale Boosting Strategies Workshop 2. **Beginning Teachers:** Classroom Management Essentials Workshop 3. **Seasoned Teachers:** Renewing Passion in Teaching Retreat
	Semester 1	1. **Administrators:** Cultivating a Positive School Culture Training 2. **Beginning Teachers:** Differentiated Instruction Techniques Training 3. **Seasoned Teachers:** Advanced Strategies for Teacher Well-Being Workshop
	Semester 2	1. **Administrators:** Empathetic Leadership and Support Seminar 2. **Beginning Teachers:** Building Rapport With Students Seminar 3. **Seasoned Teachers:** Cultivating Resilience in Experienced Educators Seminar

TABLE 8.4: EXAMPLE 2: TIMELINE AND MILESTONES FOR PROFESSIONAL DEVELOPMENT INTERVENTION

ISSUE	SEMESTER	MILESTONES, PD STRANDS, AND INTERVENTIONS
Limited Student Engagement	**Summer**	1. **Administrators:** Understanding Factors That Promote Student Engagement Workshop 2. **Beginning Teachers:** Understanding Factors That Promote Student Engagement Workshop 3. **Seasoned Teachers:** Advanced Strategies for Student Engagement Workshop
	Semester 1	1. **Administrators:** Engagement Strategies Across the Curriculum Workshop 2. **Beginning Teachers:** Engagement Strategies Across the Curriculum Workshop 3. **Seasoned Teachers:** Incorporating Technology for Enhanced Student Engagement Training

TABLE 8.5: EXAMPLE 3: TIMELINE AND MILESTONES FOR PROFESSIONAL DEVELOPMENT INTERVENTION

ISSUE	SEMESTER	MILESTONES, PD STRANDS, AND INTERVENTIONS
Low Reading Scores	**Summer**	1. **Administrators:** Comprehensive Literacy Intervention Workshop 2. **Beginning Teachers:** Foundational Literacy Instruction Workshop 3. **Seasoned Teachers:** Advanced Literacy Strategies for Seasoned Teachers
	Semester 1	1. **Administrators:** Targeted Reading Strategies Seminar 2. **Beginning Teachers:** Strategies for Supporting Struggling Readers Seminar 3. **Seasoned Teachers:** Tailored Interventions for Diverse Learners Workshop
	Semester 2	1. **Administrators:** Fostering a Reading Culture Training 2. **Beginning Teachers:** Cultivating a Reading Community Session 3. **Seasoned Teachers:** Fostering a Reading Culture in Experienced Classrooms Workshop

Establishing a Timeline With Milestones for Implementation

Some teaching teams will articulate numerous PD interventions and solutions during the action planning process. Or they want to implement innovative teaching strategies requiring time to build expertise, like improving reading (see Table 8.5). It'll likely overwhelm them and the teaching staff if they try to implement every intervention simultaneously. Creating a timeline with milestones can streamline the implementation path in spaces looking to improve several facets of their instruction. Timelines enable teaching teams to set the progression of interventions at a level that allows them to build capacity within the teaching staff—each intervention serving as a building block.

As mentioned in Chapter 6 on page 93, action plans are a form of project management. Among several key things, action plans establish timelines for tasks and solutions (Bridges, 2024). To set timetables for solutions (see Tables 8.3, 8.4, and 8.5), timelines are visual and strategic tools teams use to prioritize tasks, track progress, and focus communication (Sambol, n.d.).

As your team begins implementing data-driven PD interventions, it's critical to prioritize the needs identified with teaching staff members' capacity. I suggest strengthening their core instruction (see Chapter 3) as a foundation for proceeding with innovative teaching strategies. This means reconciling the various solutions to ensure interventions can be carried out effectively, logically, and coherently. This can be done by establishing a detailed timeline with milestones and setting endpoints based on semesters or dates. See Tables 8.3, 8.4, and 8.5 for examples of how timelines can be structured in action plans by semester. Feel free to use dates instead.

Identifying Internal and External Talent for Facilitating PD Interventions

Ideally, your teaching staff or team members should be able to provide the talent to assist the teaching team with PD interventions (Darling-Hammond et al., 2017). It's essential to begin internally because it honors in-house expertise. If we don't allow opportunities for our passionate teachers to bloom and fail forward, we will most likely lose our talented teachers. They will go elsewhere, to places that provide them more room to grow professionally. Besides, how else will they get the experiences they need to learn and grow?

In my case that's what happened to me. As I developed myself as a PD facilitator, I began getting pushback from my director and lateral colleagues, eventually causing me to take and grow my abilities elsewhere. It wasn't an easy decision because I loved my colleagues and school district. Once I realized that I couldn't contribute to the team's mission and goals using my honed expertise, it became easier to leave. Unfortunately, during my travels, I see a lot of this happening to talented and passionate educators in schools nationwide. Teaching teams, honor your folks and help them grow as PD facilitators if they request you to do so.

However, there are times when no one in your school will have the expertise to carry out the PD interventions, especially those requiring several dates to implement (see Tables 8.3, 8.4, and 8.5). Your teaching team will now have to seek outside expertise. First, look within your school system or region; hiring an outside consultant will be necessary if that person(s) doesn't exist locally. You'll have to gain approval and funding from whoever does so in your school or district—so be sure to follow whatever that process entails. There isn't a handbook for hiring coaches and consultants. However, based on our combined experiences, here are some qualities teaching teams can look for in a PD provider(s):

1. **Expertise and Experience:** Seek out a consultant(s) with expertise in the specific instructional or skills-based area(s) relevant to the teaching team's needs. Experience delivering successful PD in this area(s) demonstrates the consultant's ability to understand and address challenges effectively (Dedering et al., 2015).
2. **Evidence-Based Practices:** Seek consultants who base their coaching and PD interventions on theory, research-backed methodologies, and sound practices that work in education. Ideally, seek someone who can facilitate the same learning experiences your teachers will implement with students (Darling-Hammond et al., 2017). They should be able to provide evidence (receipts) of successfully implementing the strategies you're hiring them for. Teaching teams should prioritize individuals who understand instructional innovation through an action research process.
3. **Customization and Flexibility:** Strong consultants and PD providers will know how to tailor their canned services to meet your school's unique needs and context. They must be flexible enough to adapt their approach based on your feedback and evolving circumstances (Alessandra, 2024).
4. **Engagement and Communication Skills:** Effective coaches must have strong communication and facilitation skills to engage participants and create a positive culture and learning environment (Alberts, 2024). They must also convey complex concepts effectively and inspire active participation through interactive and reflective activities. When vetting prospects, watch online videos and ask for recommendations from trusted colleagues.
5. **Track Record of Success:** Seek out consultants with a track record of success in improving outcomes for participants and schools they've coached at (receipts). Receipts can come from case studies from their professional experience and testimonials or references from previous or current clients.
6. **Collaborative Approach:** Seek collaborative coaches who will work closely with your teaching team to understand your goals, challenges, and school culture (CoachHub, 2023). They should be willing to collaborate with you to customize the PD interventions.
7. **Support and Follow-Up:** Instructional innovation is continuous. PD interventions will most likely be implemented using strands and milestones. Hire consultants who can provide the ongoing support, resources, and follow-up your teaching team needs to sustain solutions (Centers for Disease Control and Prevention [CDC], 2024).

By carefully considering these qualities and attributes when selecting the right consultant(s) to collaborate with your teaching team, you can ensure you're investing in a partner who can help support your team's action plan effectively.

Chapter Summary

Chapter 8 guides teaching teams through refining action plans by planning the implementation of their data-driven PD interventions, categorizing them into strands, and setting milestones. This chapter encourages and models tips for tailoring PD to administrators, beginning teachers, and experienced teachers' unique needs. Moreover, guidance for establishing timelines with milestone markers by semester or dates to address solutions systematically is emphasized.

The distinction between PD interventions and solutions is clarified, emphasizing that interventions serve as tools to support solution implementation. The chapter also expands on level-setting data-driven PD interventions and emphasizes the need to utilize multiple metrics to tailor the right interventions for schools. Engaging in the action research process prescribed here allows teaching teams to make evidence-based decisions, track progress, and strategically adapt instructional strategies.

Furthermore, this chapter encourages teaching teams to seek the right internal talent and external collaborators to facilitate their PD interventions effectively. Additionally, the chapter provides guiding principles for choosing the right coach and consultants for PD interventions, stressing the importance of collaborative, customized approaches prioritizing ongoing support and follow-up. The information provided here segues nicely into our final chapter on implementing data-driven PD and Step 5 of our instructional innovation model.

Reflective Prompts for Individual Teaching Team Members

1. Reflect on your previous experience in setting PD strands and implementation milestones. Did the process outlined throughout this chapter clarify and evolve your understanding of the value of differentiating PD strands for administrators, beginning teachers, and seasoned teachers? What are your specific takeaways?
2. Reflect on your ability to facilitate any PD interventions identified by teaching the team successfully. How does your previous experience qualify you to lead a PD intervention successfully with select teachers at your school?
3. What steps can you take to enhance your ability to coach teachers effectively at your school? What successful strategies have you implemented with students that you can adapt for adults, empowering them in their professional growth?

Reflective Prompts for Teaching Teams

1. How can you teaching team streamline mapping the PD strands and milestones process? What does your team need to know and do to chart a linear path for PD interventions within your action plan?
2. Reflect on the PD interventions your team has set strands and milestones for. Which internal colleague can successfully facilitate any of the interventions?
3. Reflect on the PD interventions your team has set strands and milestones for. Which coach, consultant, or PD provider is the team aware of who has a track record and could effectively facilitate any of the interventions? Which lateral colleagues can you tap for advice on seeking the right collaborator(s)?

CHAPTER 9

Step 5: Implementing Data-Driven Professional Development

In this final chapter and final step of the instructional innovation process, teaching teams learn the importance of effective professional development (PD) by examining the relevant literature. Teams then focus on implementing each PD strand and milestone they developed in Chapter 8. After delivering PD activities, they collect relevant data from participants to evaluate the effectiveness of their prescribed interventions. Creating effective feedback instruments, such as mixed-methods surveys, provides teaching teams with valuable insights into participants' perceptions of PD experience and motivations of resistant colleagues.

Additionally, typed questionnaires are employed to assess improvement in content knowledge. Teams learn the best ways to analyze the collected data and look for emerging themes and patterns that will inform future PD solutions. By doing this, they ensure continuous improvement and alignment with the identified areas of teaching needing enhancement. Active evaluation of the effectiveness of the implemented PD and utilizing data-driven insights help teams strengthen the impact of their PD efforts during the instructional rounds.

The Importance of Effective Professional Development

Creating effective PD is an essential payoff to the action research process for teaching teams. It can also make or break the credibility of the instructional innovation process with their colleagues. Getting this part right is so critical that I would be remiss not to mention Laura Desimone and her influential contributions to the knowledge of effective PD and teacher mentoring (University of Delaware, 2025).

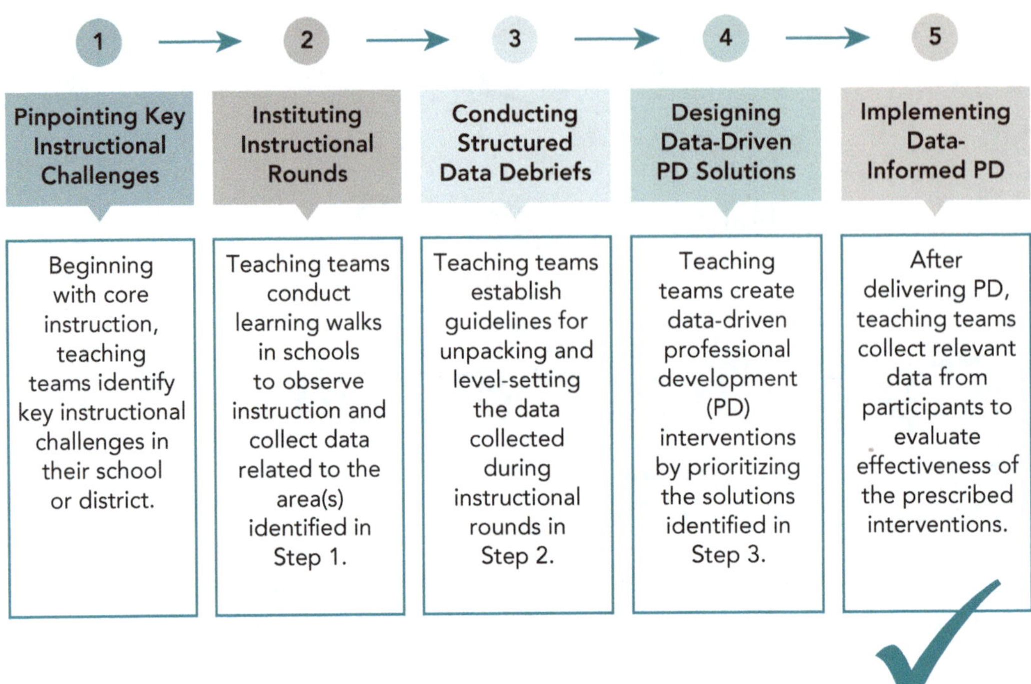

Desimone's work emphasizes the importance of using empirical methods to assess professional development, focusing on a comprehensive framework and outcomes such as teacher learning, changes in instructional practices, and, ultimately, student achievement (Desimone & Garet, 2015).

In her earlier work, Desimone (2009) emphasized that the realization of educational reform depends on effective teacher PD, leading to better learning experiences and academic achievement for students. However, all PD is not created equal. If teachers continue to struggle with appropriate pedagogical strategies for daily teaching following PD, their facilitation will not positively impact outcomes for all students. Moreover, not receiving effective PD causes frustration and negatively impacts the attitudes of teachers. The effectiveness of PD depends on the interaction and confluence of teachers' knowledge and beliefs to improve the content and pedagogy of their instruction (Desimone & Phillips, 2013). To be effective, PD must be data driven.

Defining Data-Driven Professional Development

Data-driven PD is an approach where decisions about the PD of teachers and instructional leaders supporting them are informed by data analysis (Hirsch et al., 2018). By now, teaching teams understand that the advice and processes in this book are entirely data driven—not leaving anything to chance. Each team member has learned that instructional innovation is a continuous, never-ending process that engages them as both researchers and practitioners. Possessing the necessary theoretical and experiential backgrounds is a powerful way to collectively implement PD interventions and progress toward the right solutions for their schools. Here are some key aspects of data-driven PD:

1. **Data Collection:** Teaching teams gather data about teaching at their school from several sources, including student and teacher assessments and classroom observations (Valenzuela, 2022j).
2. **Data Analysis:** Teaching teams analyze the collected data to identify areas of strength, improvement, and trends in teaching and learning (Valenzuela, 2022j).
3. **Goal Setting:** Teaching teams set specific, measurable, achievable, relevant, and time-bound goals for growing teachers and positive student outcomes. Many professionals commonly use such SMART goals to provide a road map to their aspirations (Leapsome Team, n.d.).
4. **PD Planning:** Teaching teams develop PD interventions tailored to address the areas of improvement. These activities include personalized workshops, coaching, collaborative lesson design, and peer observation using learning walks. Strands, milestones, and timelines are set in this phase (Valenzuela, 2022j).
5. **Implementation, Evaluation, and Adjustment:** Teaching teams assess the effectiveness of their PD interventions, analyzing their impacts on teaching practice and learner outcomes. This analysis provides valuable insights that guide the adjustment of PD interventions based on feedback and new learning (Valenzuela, 2022j).

The data-driven PD process is not a onetime event but a continuous cycle that teaching teams can use to make evidence-based decisions to improve teaching and learning in their schools. This process can ensure a dynamic and responsive approach to professional learning for teaching professionals. Moreover, I've defined data-driven PD and reiterated the key aspects mentioned in previous chapters for leveraging data for PD interventions. Getting this far in the pages of this book, teaching teams now have a solid foundation in data collection, analysis, setting solutions, and PD intervention planning. After reading the subsequent sections of this chapter, they will be fully prepared to effectively implement the PD interventions using the PD strands, milestones, and timelines articulated in their action plans (see Chapter 8).

Developing and Implementing Professional Development Strands, Milestones, and Timelines

School systems and districts typically set in-service days for PD. In our experience, teachers and administrators often receive blanket PD with little personalization. This does very little to create teacher buy-in—making in-service days ritualistic and much wasted time they could have spent setting up or working in their classroom.

Instructional innovation through action research processes is all about personalizing PD interventions for administrators, beginning teachers, and seasoned educators. See Chapter 8 (page 127) for an explanation and Tables 8.2 (page 127) and 9.1 for multiple examples and additional insights into specific PD intervention strands. Moreover, implementation of PD strands, milestones, and timelines doesn't necessarily have to occur solely on districtwide in-service days. Instead, PD treatments can be flexible and carried out during common planning time, teaching team meetings, or one-to-one. Implementing PD treatments throughout the daily routines of the school calendar year can allow for greater customization and foster a culture of continuous learning and collaboration between educators.

TABLE 9.1: TARGETED PROFESSIONAL DEVELOPMENT INTERVENTION STRANDS

PD INTERVENTION	ADMINISTRATOR STRAND	BEGINNING TEACHER STRAND	SEASONED TEACHER STRAND
Project-Based Learning (PBL)	1. Leadership skills in supporting PBL implementation 2. Culture-building strategies for PBL classrooms 3. Intensive instructional coaching techniques in projects	1. Introduction to PBL major concepts and practices 2. Practical application of PBL with diverse learners 3. Scaffolding the project process	1. Advanced PBL techniques and tech integration 2. Mentoring newbies in PBL implementation 3. Flexible grouping in PBL
Common Assessments	1. Instructional coaching techniques for assessment 2. Aligning assessments with curriculum standards 3. Effectively utilizing assessment data to inform instructional decisions	1. Assessment fundamentals 2. Implementing formative and summative assessments 3. Assessment strategies for diverse learners	1. Advanced assessment analysis 2. Peer collaboration for assessment 3. Leadership in assessment design and implementation

Timelines for PD interventions can be set by semesters, beginning with the summer since that marks the start of the school year. Of course, schools can opt to use dates instead of semesters if they prefer. See Tables 8.3 (page 128), 8.4 (page 129), 8.5 (page 129), 9.2, and 9.3 for respective examples of timelines and milestones for PD interventions ranging from issues that include poor teacher morale, waning student engagement, low reading scores, improvements to the implementation of project-based learning (PBL) and common assessments. I felt it critical to provide teaching teams with multiple examples of setting timelines and milestones for PD interventions.

TABLE 9.2: EXAMPLE 1: TIMELINE AND MILESTONES FOR PROFESSIONAL DEVELOPMENT INTERVENTION

PD INTERVENTION	SEMESTER	MILESTONES, PD STRANDS, AND INTERVENTIONS
Project-Based Learning (PBL)	**Summer**	1. **Administrators:** Leadership skills in supporting PBL implementation 2. **Beginning Teachers:** Introduction to PBL major concepts and practices 3. **Seasoned Teachers:** Advanced PBL techniques and tech integration
	Semester 1	1. **Administrators:** Culture-building strategies for PBL 2. **Beginning Teachers:** Practical application of PBL with diverse learners 3. **Seasoned Teachers:** Mentoring newbies in PBL implementation
	Semester 2	1. **Administrators:** Intensive instructional coaching techniques in projects 2. **Beginning Teachers:** Scaffolding the project process 3. **Seasoned Teachers:** Flexible grouping in PBL

TABLE 9.3: EXAMPLE 2: TIMELINE AND MILESTONES FOR PROFESSIONAL DEVELOPMENT INTERVENTION

PD INTERVENTION	SEMESTER	MILESTONES, PD STRANDS, AND INTERVENTIONS
Common Assessments	**Summer**	1. **Administrators:** Instructional coaching techniques for assessment 2. **Beginning Teachers:** Assessment fundamentals 3. **Seasoned Teachers:** Advanced assessment analysis
	Semester 1	1. **Administrators:** Aligning assessments with curriculum standards 2. **Beginning Teachers:** Implementing formative and summative assessments 3. **Seasoned Teachers:** Peer collaboration for assessment
	Semester 2	1. **Administrators:** Effectively utilizing assessment data to inform instructional decisions 2. **Beginning Teachers:** Assessment strategies for diverse learners 3. **Seasoned Teachers:** Leadership in assessment design and implementation

The following vignette by Assistant Director of Magnet Schools Drew Hirshon in Colorado's Pueblo School District 60 shares insights into a teaching team working through the process of developing and implementing a timeline and milestones for PD interventions for a PBL initiative. See Table 9.2 for the detailed timeline and milestones.

After establishing robust core instruction, a teaching team in a high school in Pueblo, Colorado, implemented an initiative to refine and enhance their innovative teaching with PBL practices. Recognizing the limitations of the blanket PD they previously implemented for all staff, they utilized a more personalized and structured approach to carrying out their action plans. They sought to implement targeted and flexible interventions by collectively mapping out what aspects of PBL they wanted the school's instructional leaders to support and which aspects of PBL they knew were best for both beginning and seasoned teachers to learn and facilitate with students. While creating the timeline and milestones for PBL PD interventions, they utilized a thought partner from a neighboring school system that had already successfully implemented PBL in three schools. Enlisting this assistance helped them fill their knowledge gaps during the ideation process.

During the summer, administrators focused on improving their leadership skills in supporting PBL implementation. Beginning teachers were introduced to the major PBL concepts and practices, while seasoned teachers delved into advanced projects integrating artificial intelligence (AI) tools for the development of more real-world student products. During the first semester, administrators concentrated on supporting culture-building strategies for PBL, setting the tone for a more collaborative schoolwide environment. Beginning teachers began applying the PBL practices they learned with classes, gaining experience, and receiving feedback. Seasoned teachers took on mentoring roles utilizing learning walks to provide feedback to their colleagues implementing projects for the first time.

As all levels increased their capacity due to the previous interventions, more intensive coaching began in the second semester for administrators to support teachers' project processes and encourage flexible grouping for seasoned folks. Creating and implementing this comprehensive and semester-based PD plan, prioritizing continuous learning and collaboration, nurtured a culture of innovation and effective PBL practices within the school. ●

Implementing Professional Development Strands, Milestones, and Timelines

Consider your milestones as goals your teaching team sets. PD interventions, although separate events, are markers (milestones) along your path to achieving the solutions the team set in action plans. Additionally, PD interventions have prescribed goal-attainment steps. As a reminder, there is no shame in consulting experienced thought partners in determining and organizing the PD strands. It's always best to seek counsel from others who have already accomplished what the teaching teams seek to accomplish.

I highly recommend making your PD sessions outcomes based. Use conversational language; don't make each outcome exceptionally long by being too text heavy. I always share with participants no more than two or three outcomes they'll leave our session with. Here's an example of my favorite participant outcomes to facilitate:

1. Learn to nurture critical thinking through reflective prompts and strategies promoting engagement.
2. Discover skills to make our thinking visible.
3. Explore the essential behaviors that enable students' readiness for effective learning.

Ensure sessions are at most 90 minutes and allow participants to focus on each intended outcome. Provide explanations, modeling, time to learn and practice, and actionable resources for each outcome. Facilitate PD sessions using replicable protocols they can use later in their classrooms and create a virtual repository of resources they can always refer back to in their own learning.

Data collection after each PD intervention is a critical component of this data-driven process. It helps teaching teams understand the effectiveness of their interventions and the intrinsic motivation of their colleagues, especially the resistant ones they will undoubtedly encounter throughout this process. With resistant colleagues becoming more prevalent in today's post-COVID-19 educational landscape (Valenzuela, 2024b), let's take a moment to understand the importance of deciphering the intrinsic motivations of the colleagues you're working to impact along with solid steps for doing so.

Navigating Resistance and Overcoming Challenges in Professional Development

Building relationships and rapport with the teachers teaching teams work with is critical to implementing PD interventions. Sometimes, despite our best efforts, some colleagues will push back. As discussed in Chapter 1 (page 19), resistant colleagues can significantly undermine and challenge the team's effectiveness. Their words and actions often suggest opposition to change, unwillingness to collaborate, or disruptive attitudes. However, it's important not to lose hope in the team's instructional innovation pursuits or dismiss challenging colleagues altogether. Remember, boosting collective teacher efficacy does wonders for empowering teams to accomplish excellent outcomes for students (Hattie, n.d.).

To gain deeper insight into why some of our colleagues resist school transformation, let's delve into the role perceptions and self-efficacy play in shaping intrinsic motivation. Understanding the underlying factors causing their behaviors and intrinsic motivations is critical to the teaching team's success and lays the groundwork for fostering and developing meaningful professional interactions. Because PD interventions are data driven, you'll get the data you need to act accordingly.

Exploring Connections Perceptions and Self-Efficacy of Resistant Colleagues

Intrinsic motivation drives individuals to engage in activities for satisfaction and enjoyment rather than external rewards (Di Domenico & Ryan, 2017). Keen teaching teams take the time to understand the inherent motivations of their divisive colleagues by surveying their perceptions and self-efficacy beliefs. Exploring educators' perceptions and self-efficacy is critical in academic research for many reasons, such as understanding behavior and intrinsic motivations (Barni et al., 2019) for teaching.

Perceptions refer to teachers' beliefs, attitudes, and opinions about their students, teaching practices, and school environment. They are the lens through which teachers find meaning and navigate their teaching role—impacting their instructional decisions and the dynamics of their classroom environment (G. Thompson & Harbaugh, 2013).

For example, your school's teaching team begins an initiative to implement instructional rounds (Valenzuela, 2024a) and wants to build trust and collaboration with the teaching staff. Here are two sample survey questions that teaching teams can adapt to gain perspective on perceptions.

1. I perceive instructional rounds as a supportive process rather than an evaluative one.

2. I believe instructional rounds can be a valuable addition to our school's efforts to improve learning outcomes.

Self-efficacy is a concept proposed by psychologist Albert Bandura (1977) in his seminal work. Bandura's self-efficacy theory suggests that people's confidence in their abilities can significantly impact their internal motivation and good decision-making skills. Individuals with higher self-efficacy levels tend to experience lower stress levels and learn to cultivate a positive outlook on what is ahead of them (Cherry, 2024).

Here are two sample survey questions that teaching teams can adapt to gain perspective on self-efficacy beliefs.

1. I feel confident in my ability to participate effectively in instructional rounds.
2. I am open to participating in instructional rounds as a means of professional development.

Using ChatGPT, I developed a sample Instructional Rounds Perception Survey. (I edited the items to remove inaccurate material.) Teams can adapt it for specific PD interventions.

INSTRUCTIONAL ROUNDS PERCEPTION SURVEY

https://bit.ly/402sOO4

Since both perceptions and self-efficacy beliefs significantly impact motivation and how people behave, researchers survey both aspects to understand the actions and behaviors of participants better. In the context of instructional innovation for this book, teaching teams act as both practitioners and researchers driven to understand and enhance behavior and team collaboration—especially when engaging resistant colleagues. Through this dual lens, teaching teams can unpack how the resisters to the transformation required for instructional innovation perceive their school environment, their colleagues, and the effectiveness of PD interventions.

Doing so can help teaching teams gain insight into how the resisters to change perceive their teaching roles and capabilities, providing the underlying causes of their resistance. This insight is paramount in using the information we collect during the upcoming implementation of PD interventions, empathetic responses, and targeted approaches to overcoming resistance and becoming collaborative for nurturing transformation within schools.

Approach to Data Collection and Analysis Following Professional Development Interventions

As seen in the previous section, data collected following PD interventions differ from those your teaching team collected and analyzed in Chapters 6 and 7 following the learning walks. That's because you'll survey participants after implementing each PD intervention in your strands and milestones instead of jotting down notes after observing them. Although both methods provide data points, the purpose and data type differ.

The data the team collects following PD interventions is used to evaluate effectiveness. These data collections should focus on your participants' attitudes, perceptions, and self-efficacy beliefs. I highly recommend utilizing survey instruments that allow for mixed-methods adoption to collect both quantitative and qualitative data for the team to analyze. *Mixed methods* refers to a research approach in which the researchers analyze both quantitative and qualitative data within the same study (Shorten & Smith, 2017). It's also important to note that some teaching teams may also choose to evaluate the effectiveness of PD, by gathering classroom observation and student learning data. Gaining an understanding of how students are receiving instruction is also helpful for making PD data driven.

Quantitative data include anything that can be counted, measured, or given a numerical value and are represented numerically (National Library of Medicine, 2022a). Qualitative data represents information and concepts not defined by numbers (National Library of Medicine, 2022b). Survey instruments will be used to capture your data acquired through mixed methods in a structured process and prepare them for analysis.

Survey Instruments

Survey Instruments collect data through structured questions on a five-point Likert scale administered to participants to measure their opinions, beliefs, and experiences following a PD intervention. For the surveys your teaching team will develop and use, the Likert scale will range from *strongly disagree* to *strongly agree*, with three gradations in between: *disagree*, *neutral*, and *agree*. Responses are assigned numerical values, ranging from 1 to 5, to allow for quantitative data analysis (QuestionPro, 2025).

I recommend that your surveys also include qualitative components. Including open-ended questions alongside the Likert scale questions allows participants to provide detailed narrative responses, which offer additional insights into their perspectives and reasons for their quantitative ratings (Amberscript, 2023). For the ease of getting collective and individual data points for participants, I recommend administering and collecting data from your instruments using Google Forms (Chandola, n.d.). See Figure 9.1 for an example of a survey question using a five-point Likert scale and open-ended question administered on a Google Form.

FIGURE 9.1: PERCEPTIONS SURVEY QUESTION USING A FIVE-POINT LIKERT SCALE AND OPEN-ENDED QUESTION FOLLOWING PROFESSIONAL DEVELOPMENT INTERVENTION—RELEVANCE

How would you rate the relevance of today's professional training to your teaching role? (1 = *low relevance*, 5 = *high relevance*)

1 2 3 4 5

What aspects of today's professional training do you feel particularly enhance your teaching?

____

____

____

Data Evaluation

Data collection and evaluation have two main purposes: First, they seek to evaluate the effectiveness of PD interventions, and second, they seek to inform future interventions. By evaluating survey responses quantitatively following PD interventions, teaching teams can identify trends and patterns in the participants' attitudes, perceptions, and self-efficacy beliefs (see Figures 9.2 and 9.3).

FIGURE 9.2: PERCEPTIONS SURVEY QUESTION USING A FIVE-POINT LIKERT SCALE FOLLOWING PROFESSIONAL DEVELOPMENT INTERVENTION—RELEVANCE

How would you rate the relevance of today's professional training to your teaching role? (1 = *low relevance*, 5 = *high relevance*)

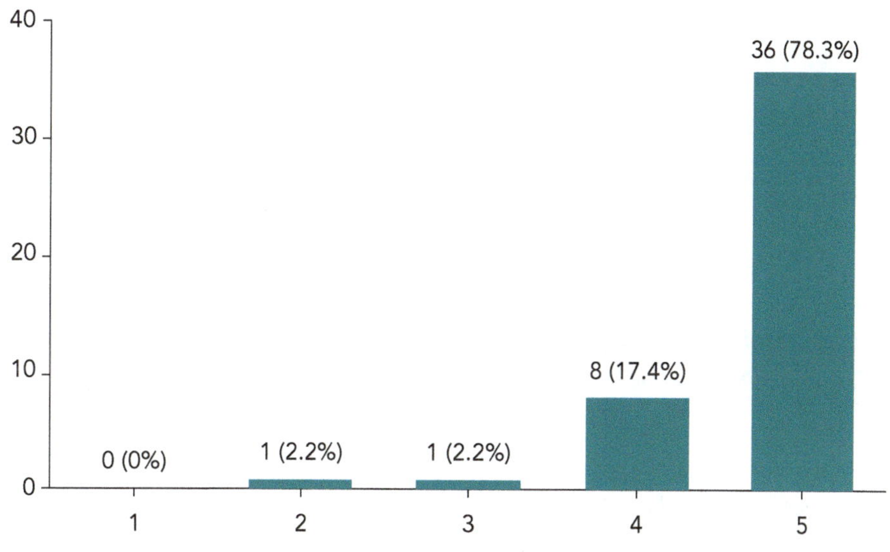

This process also involves examining their open-ended responses for themes and commonalities, which gives the teaching team insight into their experiences and perspectives. The following are some comments that participants submitted in response to the request "What aspects of today's professional training on differentiated instruction do you feel particularly enhance your teaching?" See Figure 9.1.

- *"Today's training on differentiated instruction was a game-changer. I found the strategies for adapting content, process, and product to meet diverse student needs extremely valuable. I already know my next steps to support my students' learning better."*
- *"The emphasis on understanding students' individual learning preferences stood out to me. Learning how to tailor instruction to accommodate how they learn best will undoubtedly make my teaching more effective."*

FIGURE 9.3: SELF-EFFICACY SURVEY QUESTION USING A FIVE-POINT LIKERT SCALE FOLLOWING PROFESSIONAL DEVELOPMENT INTERVENTION

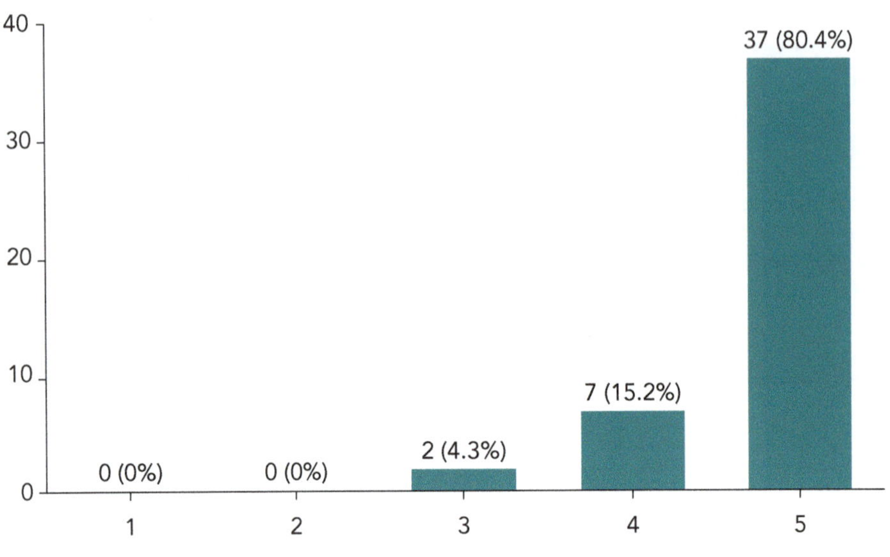

- *"I appreciated today's training's practical examples through the case studies. The relatable examples helped me visualize how to apply differentiated instruction techniques in my classroom, ensuring that all my students receive the support they need to succeed academically."*
- *"While I see some of the potential benefits of differentiated instruction, I'm hesitant about the increased workload it will entail. Balancing individualized lesson planning for a diverse classroom is challenging, especially when I don't have much free time after my teaching duties. I'll need more planning time and practical examples to begin doing this effectively."*
- *"The training reaffirmed the importance of building a supportive classroom environment where all students feel valued and capable of success. I'm excited to implement strategies such as flexible grouping and personalized learning tasks to boost my classroom culture and empower all my students."*

Common themes in these responses include the value of adapting instruction to meet students' diverse needs and appreciation for practical examples and strategies provided during the PD intervention. Resistance to the PD included concern about increased workload.

This approach provides a cyclical process and is the basis for decision making and helps the teaching team understand the data's relevance. It provides the rationale for working on existing instructional problems or identifying new ones. For resistant and struggling colleagues, taking time to understand the data enables perspective taking and empathetic responses. Moreover, being data driven becomes the basis for the team's informed decision making and adjustments to maximize the impact of their PD interventions. Imagine if every school took this approach to grow their teachers and continuously improve instruction.

Chapter Summary

This chapter closes our book by addressing the critical role of data-driven PD in driving teaching teams' instructional innovation efforts. Examining relevant literature (Desimone, 2009; Desimone & Garet, 2015), the chapter provides practical steps for designing, implementing, and evaluating PD interventions using a structured process. Examples of implementation of PD strands and milestones addressed in action plans are modeled and aligned as well. Providing the timeline and needed structure for data collection, analysis, and reflection empowers teaching teams to add more personalization and tailor interventions at their unique schools. No two schools are alike, and this data-driven approach to PD interventions honors and addresses individuality.

Moreover, PD interventions must accurately address specific instructional issues as they are, including the obstacles preventing improvement. This chapter, therefore, explores the significance of taking time to understand the perceptions and beliefs of resistant colleagues to nurture collaboration with them. Adopting mixed methods for quantitative and qualitative data collection through well-designed survey instruments allows teaching teams to evaluate the effectiveness of their PD interventions and inform decision making about future interventions. This chapter is a comprehensive guide teaching teams can refer back to for sharpening their skills for designing data-driven PD and fostering a culture of continuous learning and refinement in their school(s).

Reflective Prompts for Individual Teaching Team Members

1. Reflect on your previous experience in surveying participants following professional learning. Did you consider how their beliefs impacted their intrinsic motivation? After reading this chapter, what are your personal takeaways about the role of people's attitudes, perceptions, and self-efficacy beliefs?
2. Reflect on your ability to design effective surveys following a PD intervention. What are you looking to assess, and what are your top considerations moving forward?
3. How can responses to open-ended survey questions provide you with the beliefs and perspectives of resistant colleagues? What steps can you take to foster understanding and collaboration with them?

Reflective Prompts for Teaching Teams

1. Reflect on your teaching team's previous experience surveying participants following professional learning interventions. After reading this chapter, how will the team consider gathering insights about attitudes, perceptions, and self-efficacy beliefs when designing effective surveys?
2. When designing effective surveys following a PD intervention, how may the team design open-ended questions to gather insights about what may discourage colleagues from implementing new learning?
3. Reflecting on the teaching team's goals for each PD strand, how can you ensure that survey questions effectively capture the diverse perspectives and needs of teaching faculty?

Epilogue

Thank you for reading and implementing this book's many research-informed recommendations. *Instructional Innovation+* is a comprehensive resource that equips teaching teams with the skills, processes, tools, and protocols that promote learning and create academic and personal success for all students—especially those historically underserved (students of color and from low-income families).

Instructional innovation is not just about collecting data; it's also about teamwork, setting goals, persevering through the complexities of action research, and dedication to improving school instruction. It's a data-driven approach to instructional innovation that I hope serves you and your colleagues as much as it has done for me in my work.

Countless data collections over the years have informed the elements of the *Instructional Innovation+* model. By implementing its steps consistently and with fidelity, teaching teams can use the model to support the learning goals of all their students, especially those with diverse needs and backgrounds.

Adapting the flexible framework in Part I of this book can help develop cohesive teaching teams, improve teacher feedback cycles, and improve teaching practice by strengthening core instruction, implementing high-yielding teaching strategies, and creating instructional alignment across your school's curricula.

I urge school leaders to follow the advice in this book and acquire our sustainable *Instructional Innovation+* professional learning through Corwin for their school's teaching teams.

Doing so will ensure that instructional innovation is implemented effectively. Being effective requires collaboration, time, patience, and love. It's an investment in our teachers, students, country (wherever that may be), and humanity.

With gratitude,
Jorge Valenzuela

Appendix A
Tools and Templates

Visit the companion website to download
these tools and templates.
https://companion.corwin.com/courses/InstructionalInnovation+

Chapter 3 Resources

Project Zero thinking routines

https://bit.ly/3O75I1x

Mathematics skills integration in lessons

https://www.edutopia.org/article/5-key-building-blocks-effective-core-instruction

These resources expand on the material covered in Chapter 3 (page 47).

PBL+ Project and Performance Task Template

Title:

Content Area:

Grade Level:

Duration:

Standards to Be Assessed (3–5 standards): *Identify specific standards (such as from the Common Core State Standards or the Commonwealth of Virginia's Standards of Learning).* ***Literacy Connection(s)*** ***Numeracy Connection(s)*** ***Life Skills Connection(s)***	**Learning Intentions:** *Use student-friendly statements to identify the observable or measurable outcomes desired.*
Performance Task (Situation) or Project Description: *Describe the task(s) to be assessed. What major concept(s) will students explore, and how will they conjure a solution(s) to complete the task?*	

(Continued)

(Continued)

Product(s) and/or Performance Task: *What will students produce as evidence of attainment of learning intentions?*
Authentic Audience: *The audience comprises individuals interested in the findings and products that students create. There may be a call to action for the audience to assist with the project made by the presenter(s).*
Student Role(s): *The role(s) provides the student(s) with the opportunity to assume the career role or job associated with accomplishing the goal(s) of the project or performance task.*

Driving Question:

The unit plan's central question is used to guide students throughout the learning process.

Backward Design Alignment Tool:

Use the following Backward Design Alignment Tool, introduced in Chapter 4 (see Table 4.1), to organize formative assessments and lessons/scaffolds for each learning intention. Also, consider which learning activities align best with the intended standards and outcomes, the completion timeline, and the materials or resources students need. See a completed example in Jorge's PBL+ Project and Performance Task Exemplar. See also Table A.1 for a menu of various products that students can complete.

PRODUCT(S) AND TASKS Includes presentations, performance tasks, and summative assessments	LEARNING INTENTIONS AND PACING Includes knowledge, understanding, and skills required by students to complete products and tasks successfully	FORMATIVE ASSESSMENTS Includes both formal and informal checks of understanding to ensure students are on track with learning intentions	LESSONS, HIGH-YIELDING STRATEGIES, AND SCAFFOLDS Includes learning experiences that are closely aligned to learning intentions and formative assessments

(Continued)

(Continued)

Scoring:

Use this single-point rubric tool for scoring products and performance tasks.

EMERGING 1–3 Provide feedback for improvement	PROFICIENT 4 Grade-Level Expectations Met Provide feedback for improvement	HIGHLY PROFICIENT 5 Provide feedback for improvement	SCORE
	I have . . . (Standard #)		**/5**
	I have . . . (Standard #)		**/5**
	I have . . . (Standard #)		**/5**
	I have . . . (Standard #)		**/5**
			/20

Student Engagement and Academic Achievement Monitoring:

Monitor engagement by asking questions and leading discussions, observing participation in collaborative work by seeing how students respond in smaller settings, and polling students using engagement surveys.

Academic achievement should be monitored daily using formative assessments. Good ones for strengthening core instruction may include thumbs-up responses, exit tickets, and quizzes. Biweekly, end-of-unit and benchmark assessments are metrics your district may have in place for you to use.

Teacher Reflection:

Following implementation, consider how learning experiences can be improved in future iterations of this project.

Surveying, polling, and student conferences can help improve teaching impact. You might ask questions such as the following:

- *Which classroom activities help you learn most?*
- *What changes do you recommend I make to help you learn better?*
- *What motivates you to learn most?*
- *What can I do better?*

SOURCE: Inspired by GRASP Model by Jay McTighe. By Lifelong Learning Defined, Inc.

Jorge's PBL+ Project and Performance Task Exemplar

Title: Creating a Computer Program

Content Area: Computer Science

Grade Level: 7th Grade

Duration: 2–3 Weeks

<table>
<tr>
<td>

Standards to Be Assessed (3–5 standards):

Identify specific Standards of Learning (SOLs).

SOL Strand: Algorithms and Programming

Numeracy Connection 7.1.b

7.1: *The student will construct programs to accomplish a task as a means of creative expression or scientific exploration using block-based or text-based programming language, both independently and collaboratively,*

a. *combining control structures such as if-statements and loops including compound conditionals; and*

b. *creating clearly named variables that represent different data types, including numeric and non-numeric data, and perform operations on their values.*

Literacy Connection 7.2

7.2: *The student will document programs to make them easier to follow, test, and debug.*

</td>
<td>

Learning Intentions:

Identify the observable or measurable outcomes desired.

- **I can** develop a flowchart using step-by-step algorithms of pseudocode for my computer program.
- **I can** define and apply loops in my computer program.
- **I can** define and apply conditional logic in my computer program.
- **I can** present my program and its functionality to an audience of experts and community members.

</td>
</tr>
<tr>
<td colspan="2">

Performance Task (Situation) Description:

What is a meaningful context for students to consider in completing this task?

Students learn to use computational thinking (*decomposition, abstraction, pattern recognition, and algorithm design*) to solve computational problems in the "Computational Thinker's Project" unit plan. For this performance task, they will apply computational thinking to create an original program and teach their coding skills to an authentic audience comprised of experts and community members. To complete the task, students will interact with computer science experts, work in teams, and assume the roles of either software engineers, software developers, or programmers.

</td>
</tr>
</table>

(Continued)

(Continued)

Product(s) and/or Performance Task: *What will students produce as evidence of attainment of outcomes?* Students will create a computer program using a flowchart, loops, and conditional logic. They can choose to create their program from the following educational technology: 1. Sphero Bolt 2. littleBits Code Kit 3. ScratchJr 4. App Lab by Code.org
Authentic Audience: *The audience comprises an individual(s) interested in the findings and products that students create. They may score and or provide feedback about student performances based upon the products and presentations made.* We will invite computer science experts, community members, and other classes to view each student's performance task as a culminating event.
Student Role(s): *The Role provides the student with the opportunity to assume the career role or job associated with accomplishing the goal of the performance task.* Students may complete the performance task individually or in a team and may choose from the following three roles to complete their computer program: 1. Program Manager 2. Software Developer 3. Programmer
Student Task Instructions: *How will students complete this performance task? What activities will they do, and to which standards and outcomes are they connected? What is the timeline? What materials or resources will they need?* Use the following Backward Desing Planning Tool to organize formative assessments and lessons/scaffolds for each learning goal.
Driving Question: • How can we, as computational thinkers, design a children's video game to teach younger peers coding skills?

Backward Design Alignment Tool:

PRODUCT(S) AND TASKS Includes presentations, performance tasks, and summative assessments	LEARNING INTENTIONS AND PACING Includes knowledge, understanding, and skills needed by students to successfully complete products/tasks	FORMATIVE ASSESSMENTS Formal and informal checks of understanding to ensure students are on track with the intended learning	LESSONS, HIGH-YIELDING STRATEGIES, AND SCAFFOLDS These must be closely aligned to learning targets/objectives and formative assessments
Computer Program **2–3 Weeks**	**I can** develop a flowchart using step-by-step algorithms of pseudocode for my computer program. (2 Class Periods)	1. Flowchart summary of algorithm logic for program 2. Program rubric 3. Reflection in design journal 4. Exit ticket following daily lesson	1. Computer science guest speaker 2. Gliffy (2019) article on flowchart universal symbols using the Connect, Extend, Challenge visible thinking routine (Project Zero, 2019)
	I can define and apply loops in my computer program. (2 Class Periods)	1. Loops quiz 2. Program rubric 3. Reflection in design journal 4. Exit ticket following daily lesson	1. Computational thinking elements graphic organizer 2. Station rotations using teaching structure (e.g., Bennett, 2007) a. Coding with teacher b. Coding with a peer (pair programming) c. Individual coding 3. Programming video
	I can define and apply conditional logic in my computer program. (2 Class Periods)	1. Program rubric 2. Reflection in design journal 3. Exit ticket following daily lesson	1. Presentation rehearsal 2. Conditional logic video and simulation
	I can present my computer program and its functionality to an audience of experts and community members. (1 Class Period)	1. Presentation rubric 2. Reflection following presentation	1. Presentation rehearsal 2. Program presentation

(Continued)

(Continued)

Scoring:

What is an appropriate tool for scoring this assessment?

EMERGING 1-3 Provide feedback for improvement	PROFICIENT 4 Grade-Level Expectations Met Provide feedback for improvement	HIGHLY PROFICIENT 5 Provide feedback for improvement	SCORE
	I can develop a flowchart using step-by-step algorithms of pseudocode for my computer program. **(7.2)**		**/5**
	I can define and apply loops in my computer program. **(7.1a)**		**/5**
	I can define and apply conditional logic in my computer program. **(7.1a)**		**/5**
	I can present my computer program and its functionality to an audience of experts and community members. **(7.1a, 7.1b, 7.2)**		**/5**
Total			**/20**

Teacher Reflection: *I like how the learning took place in this project. However, next time, I will add an additional learning block or two for remediation and tiered interventions.*

TABLE A.1: EXAMPLES OF PRODUCT AND PERFORMANCE TASK TYPES

DESIGNED AND DEVELOPED	TECHNOLOGICAL	MAPPING AND PLANNING	PRESENTATION AND DEMONSTRATION	COMPOSED
Art Gallery Exhibit Garden Machine Mode of Transportation (air, land, and water) Prototype Scale Model Structure (tower, bridge, etc.) Tiny House Woodwork (benches, chairs, shelves, etc.) Working Model	Animation App Computer Program Digital Story/Comic Infographic Invention Photo Album Podcast Robot Simulation Social Media Campaign Video Virtual Museum	Blueprint Building Floorplan Business Plan Business Proposal Competitive Bid Computer Program Flow Chart Customer Estimate Design Sketch Project Management Plan Project Timeline or Timetable	Debate Lesson Facilitation Mock Trial Newscast Oral Defense Panel Discussion Performing Arts (acting, singing, and dancing) Pitch Public Demonstration Public Service Announcement Speech Spoken Word	Analysis Article Blog Brochure Call to Action Design Journal Field Guide Letter News Editorial Product Review Research Report Scientific Journal Script Training Manual

Reprinted from Valenzuela, 2023.

Flexible and Individual Grouping Options

Flexible Grouping: Flexible grouping is an instructional strategy teachers and educational paraprofessionals use. It involves periodically and strategically rearranging students into various small groups based on their learning needs, interests, and abilities. This approach allows educators to tailor instruction to meet the specific requirements of each student better, promote collaboration, and maximize learning outcomes by accommodating differences in readiness, pace, and learning styles. ***Either teachers and paras or students can lead groups.***

Individual Grouping: Individual grouping is an instructional practice employed by teachers and paras wherein each student is paired with or assigned to work independently on tasks, assignments, or learning activities that are customized to their unique strengths, weaknesses, interests, and learning goals. This approach ensures that each student receives personalized attention and opportunities to progress at their own pace while addressing their individualized learning needs.

Teacher- and Para-Led Flexible Grouping Strategies: These definitions provide a comprehensive overview of the various instructional strategies and methods teachers and paras employ in Tiers 2 and 3 to support students' learning needs and promote academic success. Strategies 1–8 can be used to help students in special education.

1. **Differentiated Instruction:** Differentiated instruction is an instructional approach where teachers and paras tailor their teaching methods and materials to accommodate the diverse learning needs, interests, and abilities of individual students or small groups within the classroom. It involves adjusting instruction content, processes, and student products to ensure all students have equitable learning opportunities and success.
2. **Skill Remediation:** Skill remediation is the targeted instruction and practice provided to students who are struggling with specific academic skills or concepts. Teachers and paras use skill remediation strategies to help students master essential skills they may have difficulty with, providing additional support and practice until proficiency is achieved.
3. **Guided Practice:** Guided practice is a teaching technique where educators provide structured opportunities for students to apply newly acquired knowledge or skills in a supportive and supervised environment. During guided practice, teachers and paras offer guidance, feedback, and assistance as students practice, ensuring they can successfully transfer what they've learned into independent work.
4. **Discussion and Questioning:** Discussion and questioning involve engaging students in thoughtful conversations and posing open-ended questions to foster critical thinking, stimulate curiosity, and deepen understanding. Teachers and paras use this method to encourage active participation, promote inquiry, and prompt students to articulate their thoughts and ideas.

5. **Assessment and Feedback:** Assessment and feedback refer to the ongoing process of evaluating students' performance and providing constructive information about their strengths and areas for improvement. Teachers and paras use various assessment methods to gauge student progress and offer feedback to guide students in enhancing their learning.

6. **Literacy Circles:** Literacy circles, also known as book clubs, are small groups of students who read and discuss the same book or text. Teachers and paras may oversee these groups, assigning roles and guiding discussions to enhance comprehension, analysis, and engagement with the text.

7. **Language Development:** Language development encompasses the process through which students acquire and refine language skills, including listening, speaking, reading, and writing. Teachers and paras use language development strategies to enhance students' linguistic proficiency and communication abilities.

8. **Feedback on Assignments:** Feedback on assignments involves providing students with constructive comments and evaluations on their work, highlighting strengths and suggesting areas for improvement. Teachers and paras offer feedback to help students refine their skills and enhance the quality of their assignments.

9. **Skill-Based Rotation:** Skill-based rotation is an instructional approach where students are grouped according to their specific skill needs within a subject or topic. Teachers and paras rotate students through different groups based on their skill levels, allowing for targeted instruction and practice.

10. **Monitoring Progress:** Monitoring progress refers to the continuous assessment of students' performance and understanding throughout a learning period. Teachers and paras regularly observe, assess, and record students' progress to inform instructional decisions and adapt their teaching strategies accordingly.

11. **Extension and Enrichment:** Extension and enrichment activities are designed to challenge and provide additional learning opportunities for students who have already mastered the core curriculum. Teachers and paras offer these activities to deepen students' understanding and foster their intellectual growth beyond grade-level expectations.

12. **Claim, Evidence, Reasoning (CER):** CER is a structured approach commonly used in scientific and argumentative writing. It involves making a clear statement or claim, supporting that claim with relevant evidence or data, and providing reasoning that explains the connection between the evidence and the claim, demonstrating the logical and scientific basis for the argument. This framework is essential for promoting critical thinking and effective communication in science and other fields where evidence-based arguments are important. For more information on CER, scan this QR code.

CLAIM, EVIDENCE, REASONING: WHAT YOU NEED TO KNOW

https://itslitteaching.com/cerwriting/

13. **Socratic Seminars:** Socratic seminars are structured discussions in which participants explore complex questions, ideas, or texts through open dialogue, critical inquiry, and thoughtful responses. Teachers and paras facilitate these discussions, guiding students to explore deeper meanings and draw connections between concepts.
14. **Project Planning and Collaboration:** Project planning and collaboration involve students working together on extended, multifaceted projects. Teachers and paras support students in planning, organizing, and executing these projects, often requiring research, teamwork, problem solving, and creative thinking.

Student-Led Flexible Grouping Strategies: These student-led flexible grouping strategies empower students to actively participate in their own learning, collaborate with peers, and develop essential skills such as critical thinking, communication, and teamwork.

1. **Peer Support and Collaboration Stations:** In this strategy, create designated "support and collaboration stations" within the classroom where students can gather in small groups to work on assignments or projects. Each station has a peer mentor who assists and guides special education students in understanding the task, breaking it down into manageable steps, and offering support as needed. This approach promotes peer support, builds social skills, and ensures that students with special needs receive personalized assistance within a collaborative learning environment.
2. **Modified Role Assignments:** Adapt role assignments to align with the strengths and abilities of special education students. Provide roles that capitalize on their individual talents, such as being the group recorder, artist, or technology expert. By assigning roles matching their abilities, special education students can actively contribute to the group's success while benefiting from the collaboration and peer interaction inherent in student-led flexible grouping.
3. **Reciprocal Teaching:** Reciprocal teaching is a strategy where students take on the role of the teacher in small-group reading sessions. Educators first demonstrate and assist students in acquiring four key strategies: summarization, question formulation, clarification, and prediction. Once students have grasped these strategies, they rotate as discussion leaders, leading conversations about the material they've read. For more information on reciprocal teaching, scan QR code, below.
4. **Collaborative Learning:** Collaborative learning is an educational approach in which students work together in small groups to achieve common learning goals. In collaborative learning, students actively engage with peers to share knowledge, solve problems, and complete tasks, fostering teamwork and collective understanding.
5. **Peer Teaching:** Peer teaching involves students taking on the role of educators to teach their peers a specific concept, skill, or topic. It encourages

RECIPROCAL TEACHING
https://bit.ly/3CsVENV

students to deepen their understanding of the material by explaining it to others and reinforces learning through teaching.

6. **Discussion and Debate:** Discussion and debate involve students engaging in conversations and arguments related to a specific topic or issue. These activities promote critical thinking, enhance communication skills, and encourage students to explore diverse viewpoints.
7. **Research and Inquiry:** Research and inquiry tasks require students to investigate a particular subject or question independently or in groups. Students gather information, analyze data, and draw conclusions, fostering independent research skills.
8. **Problem Solving:** Problem-solving tasks challenge students to identify, analyze, and solve complex problems. Students work together to explore solutions, apply critical thinking, and develop strategies to address real-world issues or academic challenges.
9. **Peer Editing and Feedback:** Peer editing and feedback involve students reviewing and providing constructive input on their peers' work, such as essays, reports, or projects. This collaborative approach helps students improve their writing and critical evaluation skills.
10. **Project Planning and Management:** Project planning and management tasks require students to organize and oversee group projects from inception to completion. They assign roles, set timelines, allocate responsibilities, and ensure the successful execution of the project.
11. **Peer Assessment:** Peer assessment involves students evaluating the work of their peers based on predefined criteria. This method encourages self-reflection, accountability, and fairness in grading or evaluating group projects.
12. **Role Assignments:** Role assignments designate specific responsibilities for each group member within a collaborative project or activity. These roles, such as leader, recorder, timekeeper, or presenter, ensure that tasks are distributed effectively.
13. **Reflection:** Reflection activities prompt students to analyze their learning experiences, identify strengths and areas for improvement, and set goals for future learning. Reflection promotes metacognition and self-awareness.
14. **Peer Support:** Peer support involves students providing emotional encouragement, motivation, and assistance to their peers. It creates a positive and supportive learning environment, fostering a sense of community and cooperation.
15. **STEM Projects:** STEM (science, technology, engineering, and mathematics) projects involve students working together on projects that require knowledge and skills from these disciplines. STEM projects encourage hands-on learning, problem solving, and innovation.

Individual Grouping Strategies: These instructional approaches involve students working independently on tasks, assignments, or learning activities customized to their unique strengths, weaknesses, interests, and learning goals. Students engage in self-directed learning, fostering autonomy and personalized skill development.

1. **Reading:** Individual reading involves students independently selecting and engaging with reading materials such as books, articles, or texts. They read at their own pace and reflect on the content to enhance comprehension and literacy skills.
2. **Journaling:** Journaling is the practice of students keeping a personal diary or record of their thoughts, experiences, and reflections. It encourages self-expression, self-awareness, and improved writing skills.
3. **Mathematics Practice:** Mathematics practice involves students independently working on mathematics problems, exercises, or assignments to reinforce mathematical concepts and improve problem-solving skills.
4. **Art Projects:** Art projects enable students to independently create visual or multimedia artwork. They explore various art forms, express themselves creatively, and develop artistic skills.
5. **Language Learning:** Language learning involves students studying and practicing a new language independently, whether through language learning apps, online courses, or textbooks. It encompasses reading, writing, speaking, and listening skills.
6. **Volunteer Work:** Volunteer work involves students participating in community service or volunteer activities independently. It fosters a sense of civic responsibility, empathy, and social awareness.
7. **Online Learning Platforms:** Online learning platforms offer students access to a variety of educational resources, courses, and materials. Students can use these platforms to explore new subjects or deepen their knowledge independently.
8. **Portfolios:** Portfolios are collections of students' work and reflections over time, showcasing their achievements and growth in various areas. They provide a means for students to track their progress and demonstrate their skills and knowledge.
9. **Research Projects:** Individual research projects assign students the task of investigating a specific topic or question independently. They gather information, analyze data, and present their findings, developing research skills and autonomy.
10. **Creative Writing:** Creative writing tasks students with crafting original stories, poems, essays, or other literary works independently. It fosters creativity, imagination, and the development of writing abilities.
11. **Science Experiments:** Individual science experiments require students to design and conduct scientific experiments or investigations independently. They gather data, analyze results, and draw conclusions, promoting scientific inquiry.
12. **Coding and Programming:** Coding and programming task students with learning computer programming languages and coding independently. They develop software applications, websites, or games, enhancing computational thinking and programming skills.

13. **Music Practice:** Music practice tasks students to independently hone their skills on a musical instrument or voice. They learn new songs, improve their technique, and express themselves through music.
14. **Personal Projects:** Personal projects are self-directed endeavors related to students' interests or hobbies. They may include activities such as gardening, cooking, photography, or model building.
15. **Critical Thinking Activities:** Critical thinking activities challenge students to engage in puzzles, brain teasers, logic games, and problem-solving exercises independently. These activities enhance analytical and critical thinking skills.

Plus/Delta Solution Chart Workshop Steps

Are Any of These Statements Currently Familiar to You?

1. "It's hard to focus on instruction when the kids' behavior is a constant concern."
2. "I feel like I'm drowning in management tasks"
3. "I'm struggling to keep up with the demands of the job."
4. "Every day feels like a new battle."
5. "I'm overwhelmed by constant new challenges."

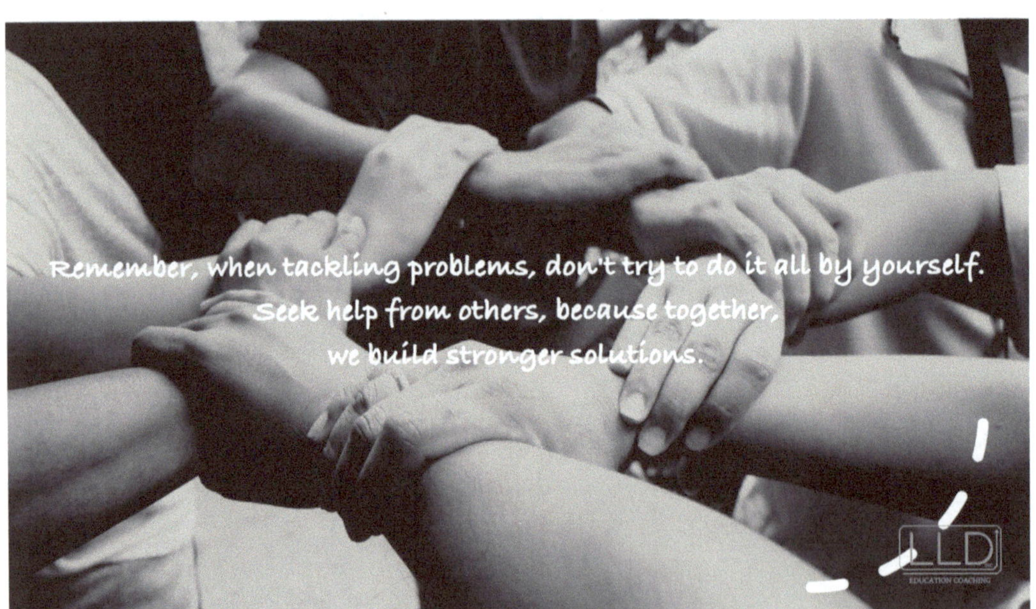

Find Some Posted Notes

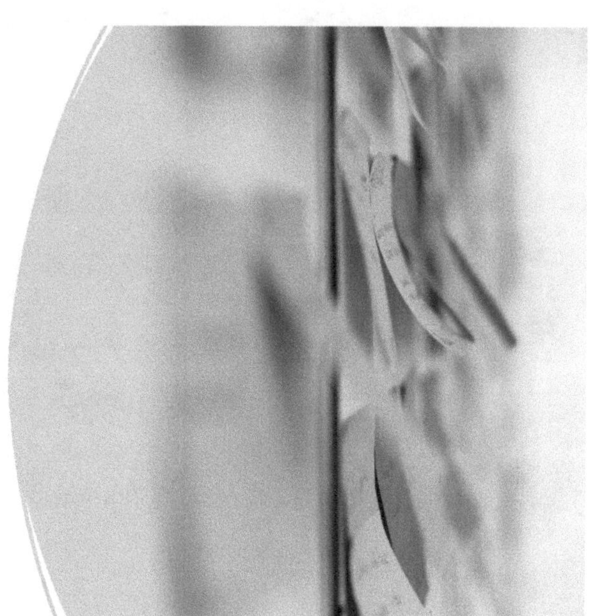

PDS Chart

Use the chart below to consider or reflect on a topic.

PLUS	DELTA

Directions

Identify two grade-level colleagues to work with.

Collaborate to develop a PDS Chart. Bring your posted notes but avoid redundancy.

Have discussions but when talking about the deltas, don't focus on solutions.

PDS Chart

Use the chart below to consider or reflect on a topic.

PLUS	DELTA	SOLUTION

Directions

1. Go to each poster and offer a solution(s)/resources per delta. (10 Mins)
2. Reconvene with your team and discuss solutions. (5 Mins)
3. Reflection (5 Mins)

Instructional Innovation+ Action Plan

Teaching Team Members:

School:

Content Area(s):

Grade Levels:

Duration: Semester 1, Semester 2, and Summer

Step 1:

Craft the Problem Statement

A good problem statement sets the stage for successful action research and guides the teaching team toward data-informed solutions tailored to their specific teaching context. We recommend teaching teams co-create and revise actionable and realistic problem statements. Problem statements should initially identify the team's current situation regarding a specific instructional problem(s), briefly describe what needs to be improved, and articulate the desired outcomes to achieve the goal(s). Problem statements can be revised at any time during the course of the action research process

Components of Improvement and Desired Outcomes

Step 2:

Analyze Learning Walk Data to Identify Instructional Issues

Revisit previously identified instructional challenges from learning walks, categorizing themes by aligning them with student outcomes or other relevant metrics (e.g., priority standards). Consider additional data points beyond learning walks, such as student performance, curriculum alignment, teacher self-assessment, and inclusivity practices, to inform the review process.

Brainstorm Interventions

Identify possible interventions to the identified instructional problems (instructional alignment, differentiation, etc.).

Prioritize Interventions

Discuss and rank the priority level for each intervention based on their impact on student outcomes and implementation feasibility. Also, identify who on the teaching staff and teaching team needs to participate in the professional development.

Highlight Positive Outcomes

Articulate the positive outcomes you hope to achieve from the successful implementation of the interventions; everyone participates.

Step 3:

Identify Potential Barriers

Identify anticipated barriers that may impede successful implementation of interventions in classrooms. Consider potential obstacles such as resistance to change, competing district initiatives, time constraints, restrictive pacing, and limited resources.

Strategies for Overcoming Barriers

Collectively offer practical strategies for overcoming the identified barriers.

Step 4:

Develop Action Plans

When refining action plans, prioritize addressing underlying problems and enhancing student success. Effective professional development (PD) interventions equip educators with transformative tools for teaching and learning. Implementing well-developed solutions enhances instructional practices and improves student learning outcomes. Teaching teams may have to seek assistance from an outside thought partner or consultant to develop logical, coherent, and sustainable action plans.

ISSUE	SOLUTIONS	POSSIBLE PD INTERVENTIONS

(Continued)

(Continued)

Step 5:

Develop Targeted Professional Development Strands

To effectively support diverse teaching staff, tailor strands for tiered curriculum design and facilitation strategies to meet the needs of administrators, beginning teachers, and seasoned teachers differently.

1. ***For Administrators:*** *Focus on nurturing a supportive environment for teacher growth. Provide PD that supports teachers' implementations with students, leadership skills, culture-building strategies, and instructional coaching techniques. Failure to develop into instructional leaders can hinder their ability to adequately support teachers.*
2. ***For Beginning Teachers:*** *Establish a strong foundation in core instruction and alignment. Offer practical PD covering rapport building, classroom management, lesson planning, and instructional strategies. Ensure PD builds foundational knowledge and practical skills.*
3. ***For Seasoned Teachers:*** *Honor their vast knowledge and experience with PD that deepens pedagogical knowledge, introduces innovative teaching strategies, and fosters reflection. Offer overview refreshers as needed, advanced content-specific sessions, peer mentoring, and leadership development opportunities.*

ISSUE	ADMINISTRATOR STRAND	BEGINNING TEACHER STRAND	SEASONED TEACHER STRAND

Step 6:

Set Timelines and Milestones

During the action-planning process, some teaching teams may propose several PD interventions or seek to implement complex teaching strategies (e.g., project-based learning), which can overwhelm both themselves and the teaching staff if attempted simultaneously. To address this, creating a timeline with milestones (completion of a PD intervention) streamlines the implementation process, allowing teams to set a progression of interventions at a manageable pace, building capacity within the teaching staff effectively.

ISSUE	SEMESTER	MILESTONES, PD STRANDS, AND INTERVENTIONS
	Summer	1. **Administrators:** 2. **Beginning Teachers:** 3. **Seasoned Teachers:**
	Semester _	1. **Administrators:** 2. **Beginning Teachers:** 3. **Seasoned Teachers:**
	Semester _	1. **Administrators:** 2. **Beginning Teachers:** 3. **Seasoned Teachers:**

Step 7:

Identify Talent for Facilitating Professional Development Interventions

It's advisable to first seek internal talent, but if needed, prioritize key qualities when selecting a consultant to support your team's professional development. Consider expertise, evidence-based practices, customization, communication skills, track record, collaboration, and ongoing support. These factors ensure effective support for your team's action plan and professional growth.

ISSUE	MILESTONES, PD STRANDS, AND INTERVENTIONS	FACILITATORS
	1. **Administrators:** 2. **Beginning Teachers:** 3. **Seasoned Teachers:**	
	1. **Administrators:** 2. **Beginning Teachers:** 3. **Seasoned Teachers:**	
	1. **Administrators:** 2. **Beginning Teachers:** 3. **Seasoned Teachers:**	

Reflect on Progress and Plan Ahead

Use this section to assess the outcomes of your action plan implementation of PD strands, milestones, and timelines. Identify areas for improvement and strategize next steps for continued growth and success.

Instructional Innovation+ Action Plan: Jorge's Exemplar

Teaching Team Members: Principal, Assistant Principal, Instructional Coach, and Lead Teacher

School: Walker Elementary

Content Area(s): English Language Arts, Mathematics, and Science

Grade Levels: 3–5

Duration: Semester 1, Semester 2, and Summer

Step 1:

Craft the Problem Statement

A good problem statement sets the stage for successful action research and guides the teaching team toward data-informed solutions tailored to their specific teaching context. We recommend teaching teams co-create and revise actionable and realistic problem statements. Problem statements should initially identify the team's current situation regarding a specific instructional problem(s), briefly describe what needs to be improved, and articulate the desired outcomes to achieve the goal(s). Problem statements can be revised at any time during the course of the action research process.

- *At Walker Elementary observable issues include poor teacher morale, limited student engagement and participation, and consistently low reading scores among third-grade students.*

Components of Improvement and Desired Outcomes

- ***Teacher morale and attitudes toward their work***
    - *Increased job satisfaction among teaching staff*
    - *Improved morale and enthusiasm in daily teaching activities*
    - *Higer retention rates of experienced teachers*
- ***Student engagement and participation in daily lessons***
    - *Increased active participation in classroom discussions and activities*
    - *Improved student interest in daily learning goals*
    - *Enhanced collaboration among students*
- ***Reading comprehension and proficiency levels among third-grade students***
    - *Higher average scores on reading comprehension assessments*
    - *Increased number of students reading at or above grade level*
    - *Improved fluency and comprehension in reading tasks*

Step 2:

Analyze Learning Walk Data to Identify Instructional Issues

Revisit previously identified instructional challenges from learning walks, categorizing themes by aligning them with student outcomes or other relevant metrics (e.g., priority standards). Consider additional data points beyond learning walks, such as student performance, curriculum alignment, teacher self-assessment, and inclusivity practices, to inform the review process.

- ***Poor teacher morale***
- ***Limited student engagement and participation***
- ***Low reading scores for third grade***

Brainstorm Interventions

Identify possible interventions to the identified instructional problems (instructional alignment, differentiation, etc.).

- ***Poor teacher morale:*** *Stress management and work–life balance training*
- ***Limited student engagement:*** *Engagement strategies workshop for elementary students*
- ***Low reading scores for third grade:*** *Foundational Literacy Workshop: Enhancing Reading Instruction for 3rd Grade*

Prioritize Interventions

Discuss and rank the priority level for each intervention based on their impact on student outcomes and implementation feasibility. Also, identify who on the teaching staff and teaching team needs to participate in the PD.

- ***Poor teacher morale:*** *Stress management and work–life balance training, Level 1 (5 teachers)*
- ***Limited student engagement:*** *Engagement strategies workshop for elementary students, Level 1 (3 teachers)*
- ***Low reading scores for third grade:*** *Foundational Literacy Workshop: Enhancing Reading Instruction for Third Grade, Level 1 (entire third-grade reading team)*

Step 3:

Identify Potential Barriers

Identify anticipated barriers that may impede successful implementation of interventions in classrooms. Consider potential obstacles such as resistance to change, competing district initiatives, time constraints, restrictive pacing, and limited resources.

- ***Poor teacher morale:*** *Resistant staff members*
- ***Limited student engagement:*** *Strict pacing*
- ***Low reading scores:*** *Time constraints*

Strategies for Overcoming Barriers

Collectively offer practical strategies for overcoming the identified barriers.

- ***Poor teacher morale:*** *Collaborative professional development and mentorship program*
- ***Limited student engagement:*** *Flexible pacing strategies, interactive and hands-on activities, and incorporation of technology and multimedia*
- ***Low reading scores:*** *Integrated reading activities, extended learning opportunities, and use of technology and digital tools*

(Continued)

(Continued)

Step 4:

Develop Action Plans

When refining action plans, prioritize addressing underlying problems and enhancing student success. Effective PD interventions equip educators with transformative tools for teaching and learning. Implementing well-developed solutions enhances instructional practices and improves student learning outcomes. Teaching teams may have to seek assistance from an outside thought partner or consultant to develop logical, coherent, and sustainable action plans.

ISSUE	SOLUTIONS	POSSIBLE PD INTERVENTIONS
Poor Teacher Morale	1. Provide struggling teachers with a support partner. 2. Create opportunities for collaborative planning. 3. Establish regular opportunities for check-ins and feedback.	1. Stress management and work–life balance training 2. Positive reinforcement and feedback strategies workshops 3. Effective communication and conflict resolution workshops
Limited Student Engagement	1. Introduce classroom projects aimed at having students explore their interests and passions. 2. Implement differentiated instruction to personalize learning for students with diverse interests and academic needs. 3. Create a positive and inclusive classroom culture that nurtures participation and peer collaboration.	1. Project-based learning and effective use of technology tools to support learning workshops 2. Training in strategies for building rapport with students 3. Workshops on student-centered teaching strategies
Low Reading Scores	1. Implement a tiered literacy program focusing on phonics, vocabulary, and reading comprehension. 2. Provide targeted tiered interventions for struggling readers. 3. Create a culture that supports reading through book clubs and reading challenges.	1. Science of reading workshops 2. Assessing student reading levels training 3. Strategies for integrating literacy across the curriculum to promote reading fluency workshops

Step 5:

Develop Targeted Professional Development Strands

To effectively support diverse teaching staff, tailor strands for tiered curriculum design and facilitation strategies to meet the needs of administrators, beginning teachers, and seasoned teachers differently.

1. ***For Administrators:*** *Focus on nurturing a supportive environment for teacher growth. Provide PD that supports teachers' implementations with students, leadership skills, culture-building strategies, and instructional coaching techniques. Failure to develop into instructional leaders can hinder their ability to adequately support teachers.*
2. ***For Beginning Teachers:*** *Establish a strong foundation in core instruction and alignment. Offer practical PD covering rapport building, classroom management, lesson planning, and instructional strategies. Ensure PD builds foundational knowledge and practical skills.*
3. ***For Seasoned Teachers:*** *Honor their vast knowledge and experience with PD that deepens pedagogical knowledge, introduces innovative teaching strategies, and fosters reflection. Offer overview refreshers as needed, advanced content-specific sessions, peer mentoring, and leadership development opportunities.*

ISSUE	ADMINISTRATOR STRAND	BEGINNING TEACHER STRAND	SEASONED TEACHER STRAND
Poor Teacher Morale	1. Morale-Boosting Strategies Workshop 2. Cultivating a Positive School Culture Training 3. Empathetic Leadership and Support Seminar	1. Classroom Management Essentials Workshop 2. Differentiated Instruction Techniques Training 3. Building Rapport With Students Seminar	1. Renewing Passion in Teaching Retreat 2. Advanced Strategies for Teacher Well-Being Workshop 3. Cultivating Resilience in Experienced Educators Seminar
Limited Student Engagement	1. Understanding Factors That Promote Student Engagement Workshop 2. Engagement Strategies Across the Curriculum Workshop	1. Understanding Factors That Promote Student Engagement Workshop 2. Engagement Strategies Across the Curriculum Workshop	1. Advanced Strategies for Student Engagement Workshop 2. Incorporating Technology for Enhanced Student Engagement Training
Low Reading Scores	1. Comprehensive Literacy Intervention Workshop 2. Targeted Reading Strategies Seminar 3. Fostering a Reading Culture Training	1. Foundational Literacy Instruction Workshop 2. Strategies for Supporting Struggling Readers Seminar 3. Cultivating a Reading Community Session	1. Advanced Literacy Strategies for Seasoned Teachers 2. Tailored Interventions for Diverse Learners Workshop 3. Fostering a Reading Culture in Experienced Classrooms Workshop

(Continued)

(Continued)

Step 6:

Set Timelines and Milestones

During the action-planning process, some teaching teams may propose several PD interventions or seek to implement complex teaching strategies (e.g., project-based learning), which can overwhelm both themselves and the teaching staff if attempted simultaneously. To address this, creating a timeline with milestones (completion of a PD intervention) streamlines the implementation process, allowing teams to set a progression of interventions at a manageable pace, building capacity within the teaching staff effectively.

ISSUE	SEMESTER	MILESTONES, PD STRANDS, AND INTERVENTIONS
Poor Teacher Morale	**Summer**	1. **Administrators:** Morale-Boosting Strategies Workshop 2. **Beginning Teachers:** Classroom Management Essentials Workshop 3. **Seasoned Teachers:** Renewing Passion in Teaching Retreat
	Semester 1	1. **Administrators:** Cultivating a Positive School Culture Training 2. **Beginning Teachers:** Differentiated Instruction Techniques Training 3. **Seasoned Teachers:** Advanced Strategies for Teacher Well-Being Workshop
	Semester 2	1. **Administrators:** Empathetic Leadership and Support Seminar 2. **Beginning Teachers:** Building Rapport With Students Seminar 3. **Seasoned Teachers:** Cultivating Resilience in Experienced Educators Seminar

ISSUE	SEMESTER	MILESTONES, PD STRANDS, AND INTERVENTIONS
Limited Student Engagement	**Summer**	1. **Administrators:** Understanding Factors That Promote Student Engagement Workshop 2. **Beginning Teachers:** Understanding Factors That Promote Student Engagement Workshop 3. **Seasoned Teachers:** Advanced Strategies for Student Engagement Workshop
	Semester 1	1. **Administrators:** Engagement Strategies Across the Curriculum Workshop 2. **Beginning Teachers:** Engagement Strategies Across the Curriculum Workshop 3. **Seasoned Teachers:** Incorporating Technology for Enhanced Student Engagement Training
	Semester 2	1. **Administrators:** 2. **Beginning Teachers:** 3. **Seasoned Teachers:**

ISSUE	SEMESTER	MILESTONES, PD STRANDS, AND INTERVENTIONS
Low Reading Scores	**Summer**	1. **Administrators:** Comprehensive Literacy Intervention Workshop 2. **Beginning Teachers:** Foundational Literacy Instruction Workshop 3. **Seasoned Teachers:** Advanced Literacy Strategies for Seasoned Teachers
	Semester 1	1. **Administrators:** Targeted Reading Strategies Seminar 2. **Beginning Teachers:** Strategies for Supporting Struggling Readers Seminar 3. **Seasoned Teachers:** Tailored Interventions for Diverse Learners Workshop
	Semester 2	1. **Administrators:** Fostering a Reading Culture Training 2. **Beginning Teachers:** Cultivating a Reading Community Session 3. **Seasoned Teachers:** Fostering a Reading Culture in Experienced Classrooms Workshop

Step 7:

Identify Talent for Facilitating Professional Development Interventions

It's advisable to first seek internal talent, but if needed, prioritize key qualities when selecting a consultant to support your team's professional development. Consider expertise, evidence-based practices, customization, communication skills, track record, collaboration, and ongoing support. These factors ensure effective support for your team's action plan and professional growth.

ISSUE	MILESTONES, PD STRANDS, AND INTERVENTIONS	FACILITATORS
Poor Teacher Morale	1. **Administrators:** Morale-Boosting Strategies Workshop 2. **Beginning Teachers:** Classroom Management Essentials Workshop 3. **Seasoned Teachers:** Renewing Passion in Teaching Retreat	1. Sara Leone 2. Jorge Valenzuela
	1. **Administrators:** Cultivating a Positive School Culture Training 2. **Beginning Teachers:** Differentiated Instruction Techniques Training 3. **Seasoned Teachers:** Advanced Strategies for Teacher Well-Being Workshop	1. Dr. Whalen
	1. **Administrators:** Empathetic Leadership and Support Seminar 2. **Beginning Teachers:** Building Rapport With Students Seminar 3. **Seasoned Teachers:** Cultivating Resilience in Experienced Educators Seminar	1. Sara Leone

(Continued)

(Continued)

ISSUE	MILESTONES, PD STRANDS, AND INTERVENTIONS	FACILITATORS
Limited Student Engagement	1. **Administrators:** Understanding Factors That Promote Student Engagement Workshop 2. **Beginning Teachers:** Understanding Factors That Promote Student Engagement Workshop 3. **Seasoned Teachers:** Advanced Strategies for Student Engagement Workshop	1. Sara Leone 2. Jorge Valenzuela
	1. **Administrators:** Engagement Strategies Across the Curriculum Workshop 2. **Beginning Teachers:** Engagement Strategies Across the Curriculum Workshop. 3. **Seasoned Teachers:** Incorporating Technology for Enhanced Student Engagement Training	1. Dr. Whalen
	1. **Administrators:** 2. **Beginning Teachers:** 3. **Seasoned Teachers:**	1. Sara Leone

ISSUE	MILESTONES, PD STRANDS, AND INTERVENTIONS	FACILITATORS
Low Reading Scores	1. **Administrators:** Comprehensive Literacy Intervention Workshop 2. **Beginning Teachers:** Foundational Literacy Instruction Workshop 3. **Seasoned Teachers:** Advanced Literacy Strategies for Seasoned Teachers	1. Sara Leone
	1. **Administrators:** Targeted Reading Strategies Seminar 2. **Beginning Teachers:** Strategies for Supporting Struggling Readers Seminar 3. **Seasoned Teachers:** Tailored Interventions for Diverse Learners Workshop	1. Dr. Whalen
	1. **Administrators:** Fostering a Reading Culture Training 2. **Beginning Teachers:** Cultivating a Reading Community Session 3. **Seasoned Teachers:** Fostering a Reading Culture in Experienced Classrooms Workshop	1. Jorge Valenzuela

Reflect on Progress and Plan Ahead

Use this section to assess the outcomes of your action plan implementation of PD strands, milestones, and timelines. Identify areas for improvement and strategize next steps for continued growth and success.

- ***Poor teacher morale:*** *Following the training, teachers reported predominantly positive Likert scale scores regarding their perceptions and self-efficacy beliefs. However, their narrative responses highlighted challenges in navigating divisive colleagues and the struggle to balance district mandates within their limited time.*
- ***Limited student engagement:*** *Post-training, teachers expressed predominantly positive Likert scale scores regarding their perceptions and self-efficacy beliefs. However, their narrative responses underscored challenges in managing students with difficult behaviors and a desire for increased support from the building administrative team.*
- ***Low reading scores:*** *Post-training, teachers expressed predominantly positive Likert scale scores regarding their perceptions and self-efficacy beliefs. However, their narrative responses emphasized the need for additional time to receive modeling and practice of the strategies learned in the workshop. They also expressed a desire to visit classrooms and observe colleagues with expertise in delivering these strategies to students.*

References

Agyapong, B., Brett-MacLean, P., Burback, L., Agyapong, V. I. O., & Wei, Y. (2023). Interventions to reduce stress and burnout among teachers: A scoping review. *International Journal of Environmental Research and Public Health*, *20*(9), 5625. https://doi.org/10.3390/ijerph20095625

Albalawi, A., & Johnson, L. N. (2022). Action research skills among public school teachers: A cross-cultural study. *International Journal of Research in Education and Science* (IJRES), *8*(2), 286–310.

Albemarle County Public Schools. (2023). *Division begins implementing instructional audit recommendations designed to close achievement gaps in reading and math.* https://www.k12albemarle.org/our-departments/communications/news-board/~board/newsroom/post/division-begins-implementing-instructional-audit-recommendations-designed-to-close-achievement-gaps-in-reading-math

Alberts, H. (2024). *The most effective relationship coaching techniques.* Quenza. https://quenza.com/blog/knowledge-base/communication-skills-coaching/

Alessandra, T. (2024). *Do you have adaptability skills?* Success. https://www.success.com/do-you-have-adaptability/

Amberscript. (2023). *Open-ended questions in qualitative research: Strategies, examples, and best practices.* https://www.amberscript.com/en/blog/open-ended-questions-in-qualitative-research/

American University School of Education. (2022). *Teacher retention: Preventing teacher turnover.* https://soeonline.american.edu/blog/teacher-retention/

Aronson, E., Blaney, N., Stephin, C., Sikes, J., & Snapp, M. (1978). *The jigsaw classroom.* Sage.

ASCD. (n.d.). *Jay McTighe.* https://www.ascd.org/people/jay-mctighe

Bandura, A. (1977). Self-efficacy: Toward a unifying theory of behavioral change. *Psychological Review*, *84*(2), 191–215.

Barni, D., Danioni, F., & Benevene, P. (2019). Teachers' self-efficacy: The role of personal values and motivations for teaching. *Frontiers in Psychology*, *10*, 1645. https://doi.org/10.3389/fpsyg.2019.01645

Bennett, S. (2007). *That workshop book.* Heinemann.

Bernat, G. B., Qualharini, E. L., & Castro, M. S. (2023). Enhancing sustainability in project management: The role of stakeholder engagement and knowledge management in virtual team environments. *Sustainability*, *15*(6), 4896.

Best Self. (2022). *How to create a safe space for deep conversations.* https://bestself.co/blogs/articles/how-to-create-a-safe-space-for-deep-conversations

Blankman, R. (2023). *Collecting data lesson plans for 1st and 2nd grade.* HMH Education. https://www.hmhco.com/blog/collecting-data-lesson-plans-1st-2nd-grade

Bondie, R. S., Dahnke, C., & Zusho, A. (2019). How does changing "One-Size-Fits-All" to differentiated instruction affect teaching? *Review of Research in Education*, *43*(1), 336–362. https://doi.org/10.3102/0091732X18821130

Boryga, A. (2023). *10 powerful ways to end your lessons.* Edutopia. https://www.edutopia.org/article/10-powerful-ways-to-end-your-lessons/

Boss, S. (2018). *3 ways to unlock the wisdom of colleagues.* Edutopia. https://www.edutopia.org/article/3-ways-unlock-wisdom-colleagues

Bowen, R. S. (2017). *Understanding by design.* Vanderbilt University Center for Teaching. cft.vanderbilt.edu/understanding-by-design

Bowen, M. (2021). *Strong core instruction: What it is and how it can address inequity and achievement gaps.* Learning Sciences International. https://www.learningsciences.com/blog/core-instruction-improve/

Bridges, J. (2024). *How to write an action plan (example included).* ProjectManager. https://www.projectmanager.com/training/make-action-plan

Bryant, J., Ram, S., Scott, D., & Williams, C. (2023). *K–12 teachers are quitting. What would make them stay?* McKinsey & Company. https://www.mckinsey.com/industries/education/our-insights/k-12-teachers-are-quitting-what-would-make-them-stay

Burns, M. (2023). *Research-backed ways to improve feedback for teachers.* Edutopia. https://www.edutopia.org/article/giving-teachers-better-feedback/

Carver-Thomas, D., & Darling-Hammond, L. (2017). *Teacher turnover: Why it matters and what we can do about it.* Learning Policy Institute. https://doi.org/10.54300/454.278

Centers for Disease Control and Prevention. (2024). *Professional development follow-up support.* https://www.cdc.gov/healthy-schools-training/about/professional-development-follow-up-support.html?CDC_AAref_Val=https://www.cdc.gov/healthyschools/tths/pd_follow_up.htm

Chandola, N. (n.d.). *How to create a Likert scale survey in Google Forms? [4 easy steps].* https://extendedforms.io/blog/create-a-likert-scale-survey-in-gforms

Cherry, K. (2024). *Self efficacy and why believing in yourself matters.* Verywell Mind. https://www.verywellmind.com/what-is-self-efficacy-2795954

City, E. A., Elmore, R., Fiarman, S., & Teitel, L. (2009). *Instructional rounds in education.* Harvard Education Press.

Clark, J. S., Porath, S., Thiele, J., & Jobe, M. (2020). *Action research.* New Prairie Press.

CoachHub. (2023). *The power of collaborative coaching: Transforming teams for success.* https://www.coachhub.com/blog/collaborative-coaching/

Communal relationships. (n.d.). In *Psychology.* iResearchNet. https://psychology.iresearchnet.com/social-psychology/interpersonal-relationships/communal-relationships/

Corwin. (2024). *Professional learning services built on impact for all learners: Visible Learning.* Sage Publications. https://www.corwin.com/professional-learning-services/key-service-lines?topic=visible-learning

Covey, S. R. (2020). *The 7 habits of highly effective people: 30th anniversary edition.* Simon & Schuster.

Cuemath. (n.d.). *Average.* https://www.cuemath.com/data/average/

Darling-Hammond, L., Hyler, M. E., & Gardner, M. (2017). *Effective teacher professional development.* Learning Policy Institute.

Dedering, K., Goecke, M., & Rauh, M. (2015). Professional background and working practices of consultants in school development: Initial empirical findings from Germany. *Journal of Educational Change, 16*(1), 27–52. https://doi.org/10.1007/s10833-014-9241-1

Desimone, L. M. (2009). Improving impact studies of teachers' professional development: Toward better conceptualizations and measures. *Educational Researcher, 38*(3), 181–199.

Desimone, L. M., & Garet, M. S. (2015). Best practices in teachers' professional development in the United States. *Psychology, Society, & Education,* 7(3), 252–263.

Desimone, L. M., & Phillips, K. J. R. (2013). Linking student achievement growth to professional development participation and changes in instruction: A longitudinal study of elementary students and teachers in Title I schools. *Teachers College Record, 115*(5). https://doi.org/10.1177/016146811311500508

Di Domenico, S. I., & Ryan, R. M. (2017). The emerging neuroscience of intrinsic motivation: A new frontier in self-determination research. *Frontiers in Human Neuroscience, 11,* 145. https://doi.org/10.3389/fnhum.2017.00145

DiSC. (n.d.). *The Five Behaviors® model for teams.* https://www.discprofile.com/fac-sup/fac-tips/model

Dyer, K. (2015). *Research proof points: Better student engagement improves student learning.* Northwest Evaluation Association. https://www.nwea.org/blog/2015/research-proof-points-better-student-engagement-improves-student-learning/

Education World. (n.d.). *Is your school culture toxic or positive?* www.educationworld.com/a_admin/admin/admin275.shtml

Edutopia. (2015). *Gaining understanding of what your students know.* https://www.edutopia.org/practice/exit-tickets-checking-understanding

Edutopia. (2018). *Learning walks: Structured observation for teachers.* https://www.edutopia.org/video/learning-walks-structured-observation-teachers/

Edutopia. (2019). *Inviting participation with thumbs-up responses.* https://www.edutopia.org/video/inviting-participation-thumbs-responses

Edutopia. (n.d.). *Formative assessment.* https://www.edutopia.org/topic/formative-assessment

Facing History and Ourselves. (2023). *Exit tickets.* https://www.facinghistory.org/resource-library/exit-tickets

Finley, T. (2015). *22 powerful closure activities.* https://www.edutopia.org/blog/22-powerful-closure-activities-todd-finley

Flip. (2024). *Streamlining instruction with Microsoft Copilot and Flip* [Video]. YouTube. https://www.youtube.com/watch?v=EMFt17D6qLI&t=393s&ab_channel=Flip

Fluency & Fitness+. (n.d.). *Measurement & data activities.* Pinterest. https://www.pinterest.com/tickledpinkinprimary/measurement-data-activities/

Formplus. (n.d.). *Formal vs. informal assessment: 15 key differences & similarities.* https://www.formpl.us/blog/formal-vs-informal-assessment

Gliffy. (2019). *Guide to flowchart symbols, from basic to advanced.* https://www.gliffy.com/blog/guide-to-flowchart-symbols

Griffith, D., & Tyner, A. (2019). *Discipline reform through the eyes of teachers.* Thomas B. Fordham Institute. https://fordhaminstitute.org/national/research/discipline-reform-through-eyes-teachers

Gruenert, S., & Whitaker, T. (2015). *School culture rewired: How to define, assess, and transform it.* ASCD.

Hagger, M. S., Rentzelas, P., & Chatzisarantis, N. L. D. (2014). Effects of individualist and collectivist group norms and choice on intrinsic motivation. *Motivation and Emotion, 38*(2), 215–223. https://doi.org/10.1007/s11031-013-9373-2

Hamilton, W., Jennings, B., & Scoggins, K. (2022). The influence of instructional rounds on teacher metacognition in a middle school context. *SN Social Sciences, 2,* 139. https://doi.org/10.1007/s43545-022-00441-5

Hanover Research. (2023). *K–12 instructional audit roadmap.* https://www.hanoverresearch.com/reports-and-briefs/k-12-instructional-audit-roadmap/?org=k-12-education

Hansen, M., & Quintero, D. (2019). *The diversity gap for public school teachers is actually growing across generations.* Brookings Institution. https://www.brookings.edu/articles/the-diversity-gap-for-public-school-teachers-is-actually-growing-across-generations/

Hartshorne, D. (2024). *How to create an action plan (with free templates and examples).* https://monday.com/blog/project-management/action-plan-template/

Haskell, J. (2013). *Working agreements.* University of Maine Cooperative Extension. https://www.uvm.edu/sites/default/files/working-agreements-defined.pdf

Hattie, J. (2009). *Visible Learning: A synthesis of over 800 meta-analyses related to achievement.* Routledge.

Hattie, J. (2012). *Know thy impact.* ASCD. https://www.ascd.org/el/articles/know-thy-impact

Hattie, J. (2023). *Visible Learning: The sequel.* Routledge.

Hattie, J. (n.d.). *Collective teacher efficacy (CTE) according to John Hattie.* Visible Learning. https://visible-learning.org/2018/03/collective-teacher-efficacy-hattie/

Heubeck, E. (2024). Few teachers learn about "science of reading" in their prep programs. Some colleges are working on that. *Education Week.* https://www.edweek.org/teaching-learning/few-teachers-learn-about-science-of-reading-in-their-prep-programs-some-colleges-are-working-on-that/2024/02

Hirsch, S., Ely, E., Lloyd, J., & Isley, D. (2018). Targeted professional development: A data-driven approach to identifying educators' needs. *School-University Partnerships, 11*(2), 84–91.

Hogan, D. (2022). *How to facilitate team work agreements: A practical, 10-step process for building a right-minded team that works as one.* Dan Hogan.

Holzer, K. (2024). *Project timeline: Meet deadlines, hit milestones, and achieve project goals.* https://www.meistertask.com/blog/project-timeline-meet-deadlines-hit-milestones-and-achieve-project-goals

Houser, K. (n.d.). *8 strategies for scaffolding instruction.* https://www.mshouser.com/teaching-tips/8-strategies-for-scaffolding-instruction

Huang, H. (2023). Stakeholder involvement in decision making: The development of a mass participation tool. *4OR-A Quarterly Journal of Operations Research, 21*, 711–712.

Hughes, W. H., & Pickeral, T. (2013). School climate and shared leadership. In T. Dary & T. Pickeral (Eds.), *School climate practices for implementation and sustainability*. A School Climate Practice Brief, Number 1, National School Climate Center. https://schoolclimate.org/wp-content/uploads/2021/05/sc-brief-leadership.pdf

Innovare. (2024). *A complete 2024 guide to data driven instruction in education*. https://innovaresip.com/resources/blog/data-driven-instruction-in-education-guide/

Institute for Research and Reform in Education. (n.d.). *Curriculum and instruction audit*. https://irre.org/services/curriculum-audit/

Jenks, A. (2010). *Richmond schools reach 100 percent accreditation*. WWBT NBC12. https://www.nbc12.com/story/13161381/richmond-schools-reach-100-percent-accreditation/

Johnson, K. G. (2016). Instructional coaching implementation: Considerations for K–12 administrators. *Journal of School Administration Research and Development, 1*(2), 37–40.

Keenan, B. (2017). *The tough work of improving school culture*. Edutopia. https://www.edutopia.org/article/tough-work-improving-school-culture-brendan-keenan/

Keenze-Wells, A. (2022). *Student behavior challenges in the way of a positive school culture*. SchoolMint. https://blog.schoolmint.com/challenges-in-the-way-of-a-positive-school-culture

Kirtman, L., & Knight-Burney, S. (2023). Educational strategies and student outcomes are not in sync. What you need to know. *Education Week*. https://www.edweek.org/leadership/opinion-educational-strategies-and-student-outcomes-are-not-in-sync-what-you-need-to-know/2023/07

Kolleck, N. (2019). Motivational aspects of teacher collaboration. *Frontiers in Education, 4*, 122. https://doi.org/10.3389/feduc.2019.00122

Kolleck, N., Schuster, J., Hartmann, U., & Gräsel, C. (2021). Teachers' professional collaboration and trust relationships: An inferential social network analysis of teacher teams. *Research in Education, 111*(1), 89–107. https://doi.org/10.1177/00345237211031585

Kuhfeld, M., Soland, J., & Lewis, K. (2022). *Test score patterns across three COVID-19-impacted school years* (EdWorkingPaper 22-521). Annenberg Institute at Brown University. https://doi.org/10.26300/ga82-6v47

Kuhfeld, M., Soland, J., Lewis, K., & Morton, E. (2022). *The pandemic has had devastating impacts on learning. What will it take to help students catch up?* Brookings Institution. https://www.brookings.edu/articles/the-pandemic-has-had-devastating-impacts-on-learning-what-will-it-take-to-help-students-catch-up/

Kunnari, I., Ilomäki, L., & Toom, A. (2017). Successful teacher teams in change: The role of collective efficacy and resilience. *International Journal of Teaching and Learning in Higher Education, 29*(2), 333–349.

Lean Construction Institute. (n.d.). *Introduction to Plus/Delta*. https://leanconstruction.org/lean-topics/plus-delta/

Leapsome Team. (n.d.). *Your complete guide to SMART goals (with examples & a free template)*. https://www.leapsome.com/blog/smart-goals

Learning Focused. (n.d.). *High yield instructional strategies 101: Exemplary schools focus on high yield instructional strategies*. https://learningfocused.com/high-yield-instructional-strategies

Lieberman, M. (2022). How school staffing shortages are hurting students. *Education Week*. https://www.edweek.org/leadership/whos-at-risk-when-schools-staffing-shortages-persist/2022/06

Marzano, R. J., Pickering, D. J., & Pollock, J. E. (2001). *Classroom instruction that works: Research-based strategies for increasing student achievement*. ASCD.

McCombes, S., & George, T. (2023). *How to write a problem statement: Guide & examples*. Scribbr. https://www.scribbr.com/research-process/problem-statement/

Medhi, B. (2024). *50 perfect messages to show appreciation for good work*. Vantage Circle. https://blog.vantagecircle.com/messages-appreciation-for-good-work/

Merrill, S. (2019). *How-to: The jigsaw method, revisited*. https://www.edutopia.org/article/how-jigsaw-method-revisited

Mertler, C. A. (2021). Action research as teacher inquiry: A viable strategy for resolving problems of practice. *Practical Assessment,*

Research, and Evaluation, 26, 19. https://doi.org/10.7275/22014442

Metcalf, T. (2015). *What's your plan? Accurate decision making within a multi-tier system of supports: Critical areas in Tier 1.* RTI Action Network. https://www.cnyric.org/tfiles/folder1306/Tier%202%20What's%20Your%20Plan.pdf

Meyer-Looze, C. L. (2015). Creating a cycle of continuous improvement through instructional rounds. *International Journal of Educational Leadership Preparation, 10*(1), 29–45.

Miller, A. (2021). *Why administrators should give feedback on assessments.* Edutopia. https://www.edutopia.org/article/why-administrators-should-give-feedback-assessments

Miro. (n.d.). *What is an action plan?* https://miro.com/strategic-planning/what-is-an-action-plan/

Monardo, J. (2017). Seeking comprehensive solutions for systemic problems in education. *Berkeley Public Policy Journal.* https://bppj.studentorg.berkeley.edu/2017/10/27/seeking-comprehensive-solutions-for-systemic-problems-in-education/

Morin, A. (n.d.). *Flexible grouping: What you need to know.* Understood for All. https://www.understood.org/en/articles/what-is-flexible-grouping

Muhammad, A. (2018). *Transforming school culture: How to overcome staff division* (2nd ed.). Solution Tree Press.

Mumford, J. M., Fiala, L., & Daulton, M. (2017). An agile K–12 approach: Teacher PD for new learning ecosystems. In C. Martin & D. Polly (Eds.), *Handbook of research on teacher education and professional development* (p. 18). IGI Global. https://doi.org/10.4018/978-1-5225-1067-3.ch020

National Center on Improving Literacy. (2022). *The science of reading: The basics.* U.S. Department of Education, Office of Elementary and Secondary Education, Office of Special Education Programs, National Center on Improving Literacy. http://improvingliteracy.org

National Education Association. (2022). *5 ways school districts can better retain educators.* https://www.nea.org/resource-library/5-ways-school-districts-can-better-retain-educators

National Library of Medicine. (2022a). *Quantitative data.* https://www.nnlm.gov/guides/data-glossary/quantitative-data

National Library of Medicine. (2022b). *Qualitative data.* https://www.nnlm.gov/guides/data-glossary/qualitative-data

National Reading Panel. (2000). *Teaching children to read: An evidence-based assessment of the scientific research literature on reading and its implications for reading instruction.* National Institute of Child Health and Human Development. https://www.nichd.nih.gov/publications/pubs/nrp/smallbook

National School Reform Faculty. (n.d.a). *Our protocols.* https://nsrfharmony.org/whatareprotocols/

National School Reform Faculty. (n.d.b). *Definitions: Protocol and activity.* https://nsrfharmony.org/in-nsrf-terms-what-are-protocols-and-activities-why-should-i-use-them/

Pak, K., Polikoff, M. S., Desimone, L. M., & Saldívar García, E. (2020). The adaptive challenges of curriculum implementation: Insights for educational leaders driving standards-based reform. *AERA Open, 6*(2). https://doi.org/10.1177/2332858420932828

Parsons, R., & Brown, K. (2002). *Teacher as reflective practitioner and action researcher.* Wadsworth/Thomson Learning.

Peanut Butter Fish Lessons. (n.d.). *4 number relationships children need to learn.* https://peanutbutterfishlessons.com/four-number-relationships/

Plotinsky, M. (2021). *4 strategies for reframing observations.* Edutopia. https://www.edutopia.org/article/4-strategies-reframing-observations

Poll Everywhere. (2020). *How to measure and ignite student engagement.* https://blog.polleverywhere.com/how-to-effectively-measure-student-engagement

Principal's Playbook. (n.d.). *Instructional rounds: Collaborative professional learning & peer feedback protocol.* https://www.theprincipalsplaybook.com/instructional-leadership/instructional-rounds-professional-learning-peer-feedback-protocol

Project Zero. (2019). *Connect, extend, challenge.* Harvard Graduate School of Education. https://pz.harvard.edu/sites/default/files/Connect%20Extend%20Challenge_0.pdf

Project Zero. (n.d.). *Thinking routines.* Harvard Graduate School of Education. https://pz.harvard.edu/projects/visible-thinking

Pyöriä, P. (2007). Informal organizational culture: The foundation of knowledge workers' performance. *Journal of Knowledge Management, 11*(3), 16–30.

QuestionPro. (2025). *Likert scale questions with examples.* https://www.questionpro.com/article/likert-scale-survey-questions.html

Reading Horizons. (2014). *What is the difference between RTI and MTSS?* https://readinghorizons.com/blog/what-is-the-difference-between-rti-and-mtss

Red Rover. (2023). *The impact of teacher absenteeism on student achievement.* https://www.redroverk12.com/blog/the-impact-of-teacher-absenteeism-on-student-achievement

Richter, D., & Pant, H. A. (2016). *Lehrerkooperation in Deutschland. Eine Studie zu kooperativen Arbeitsbeziehungen bei Lehrkräften der Sekundarstufe I.* Bertelsmann Stiftung, Robert Bosch Stiftung, Stiftung Mercator und Deutsche Telekom Stiftung.

Rinehart Kathawalla, R., & Mehta, J. (2022). Humans in hierarchies: Intergroup relations in education reform. *Educational Administration Quarterly, 58*(4), 597–637. https://doi.org/10.1177/0013161X221098072

Sackstein, S. (2016). Teachers vs educators: Which are you? *Education Week.* https://www.edweek.org/teaching-learning/opinion-teachers-vs-educators-which-are-you/2016/05

Sambol, A. (n.d.). *How to create a timeline for a project (and why they matter).* GoSkills. https://www.goskills.com/Project-Management/Resources/Project-management-timelines

Sánchez-Rosas, J., Dyzenchauz, M., Dominguez-Lara, S., & Hayes, A. (2022). Collective teacher self-efficacy scale for elementary school teachers. *International Journal of Instruction, 15*(1), 985–1002.

Sanderson, G. (2023). Seven ways to adopt a lifelong learning mindset. *The CEO Magazine.* https://www.theceomagazine.com/opinion/lifelong-learning-mindset/

Sattar, T., Ullah, M. I., & Ahmad, B. (2022). The role of stakeholders' participation, goal directness, and learning context in determining student academic performance: Student engagement as a mediator. *Frontiers in Psychology, 13*, Article 875174. https://doi.org/10.3389/fpsyg.2022.875174

Schildkamp, K., van der Kleij, F., Heitink, M. C., Kippers, W. B., & Veldkamp, B. P. (2020). Formative assessment: A systematic review of critical teacher prerequisites for classroom practice. *International Journal of Educational Research, 103*, Article 101602. https://doi.org/10.1016/j.ijer.2020.101602

Schuster, J., Hartmann, U., & Kolleck, N. (2021). Teacher collaboration networks as a function of type of collaboration and schools' structural environment. *Teaching and Teacher Education, 103*, Article 103372. https://doi.org/10.1016/j.tate.2021.103372

Shapiro, E. (n.d.). *Tiered instruction and intervention in a response-to-intervention model.* RTI Action Network. http://www.rtinetwork.org/essential/tieredinstruction/tiered-instruction-and-intervention-rti-model#top

Short, J., & Main, P. (2021). *Learning walks: A guide for school leaders.* https://www.structural-learning.com/post/learning-walks-a-guide-for-school-leaders

Shorten, A., & Smith, J. (2017). Mixed methods research: Expanding the evidence base. *Evidence-Based Nursing, 20*, 74–75.

Simons, K. H., & Simons-Zahno, J. (n.d.). *Scrum-training: Der praxisleitfaden für agile coaches.* Haufe Lexware GmbH & Co.

Sparks, S. K., & Many, T. W. (2015). *How to cultivate collaboration in a PLC.* Solution Tree. https://www.solutiontree.com/how-to-cultivate-collaboration-in-a-plc.html

Study.com. (n.d.). *How to make a budget: Lesson for kids.* https://study.com/academy/lesson/how-to-make-a-budget-lesson-for-kids.html

SurveyMonkey. (n.d.). *Top 9 student survey questions to gather feedback.* https://www.surveymonkey.com/mp/student-survey-questions/?program

TeacherVision. (n.d.). *Mini lessons and DK instant expert resources.* https://www.teachervision.com/lesson-planning/mini-lesson

Technology & Learning. (n.d.). *Robert Marzano's 9 instructional strategies.* http://edtechcoachbw.weebly.com/marzano-instructional-strategies.html

Thompson, G., & Harbaugh, A. G. (2013). A preliminary analysis of teacher perceptions of the effects of NAPLAN on pedagogy and curriculum. *Australian Educational Researcher, 40*(3), 299–314.

Thompson, J., & Xu, C. (2021). *Four types of learning walks for every school leader.* Education Elements. https://www.edelements.com/blog/four-types-of-learning-walks-for-every-school-leader

Titsworth, S., Mazer, J. P., Goodboy, A. K., Bolkan, S., & Myers, S. A. (2015). Two meta-analyses exploring the relationship between teacher clarity and student learning. *Communication Education, 64*(4), 385–418. https://doi.org/10.1080/03634523.2015.1041998

Toropova, A., Myrberg, E., & Johansson, S. (2021). Teacher job satisfaction: The importance of school working conditions and teacher characteristics. *Educational Review, 73*(1), 71–97. https://doi.org/10.1080/00131911.2019.1705247

Tschannen-Moran, M., & Hoy, A. W. (2001). Teacher efficacy: Capturing an elusive construct. *Teaching and Teacher Education, 17*(7), 783–805. https://doi.org/10.1016/S0742-051X(01)00036-1

Tutolo, N. (2017). Four steps to create a more cohesive teacher team. *Education Week.* https://www.edweek.org/education/opinion-four-steps-to-create-a-more-cohesive-teacher-team/2017/02

Tutt, P. (2022). *3 habits of highly effective teacher teams.* Edutopia. https://www.edutopia.org/article/3-habits-highly-effective-teacher-teams/

University of Delaware. (n.d.). *Laura Desimone.* https://www.cehd.udel.edu/faculty-bio/laura-desimone/

Valente, S., Lourenço, A. A., & Németh, Z. (2020). School conflicts: Causes and management strategies in classroom relationships. In M. P. Levine (Ed.), *Interpersonal relationships* (Chapter 6, pp. 79–94). IntechOpen. https://doi.org/10.5772/intechopen.95395

Valenzuela, J. (2021). *Building relationships with empathy maps.* Edutopia. https://www.edutopia.org/video/building-relationships-empathy-maps

Valenzuela, J. (2022a). *Shared agreements for working together benefit teachers and administrators.* Edutopia. https://www.edutopia.org/article/shared-agreements-working-together-benefit-teachers-and-administrators

Valenzuela, J. (2022b). *How to give teachers better feedback.* Edutopia. https://www.edutopia.org/article/how-give-teachers-better-feedback

Valenzuela, J. (2022c). *5 building blocks of effective core instruction.* Edutopia. https://www.edutopia.org/article/5-key-building-blocks-effective-core-instruction

Valenzuela, J. (2022d). *A simple, effective framework for PBL.* Edutopia. https://www.edutopia.org/article/simple-effective-framework-pbl

Valenzuela, J. (2022e). *3 ways to activate student engagement.* Edutopia. https://www.edutopia.org/article/3-ways-activate-student-engagement

Valenzuela, J. (2022f). *The post shows photographs of curriculum development from an ideation session with a teaching team.* Instagram. https://www.instagram.com/p/ChpEnhluShC/?utm_source=ig_web_copy_link

Valenzuela, J. (2022g). *A simple tool for aligning instruction and assessment.* Edutopia. https://www.edutopia.org/article/simple-tool-aligning-instruction-and-assessment

Valenzuela, J. (2022h). *Boosting critical thinking across the curriculum.* Edutopia. https://www.edutopia.org/article/boosting-critical-thinking-across-curriculum

Valenzuela, J. (2022i). *Using frequent feedback cycles to guide student work.* Edutopia. https://www.edutopia.org/article/using-frequent-feedback-cycles-guide-student-work

Valenzuela, J. (2022j). *A 5 step coaching model for instructional innovation.* Edutopia. https://www.edutopia.org/article/5-step-coaching-model-instructional-innovation

Valenzuela, J. (2022k). *Passion to purpose 5-step organizer.* Edutopia. https://wpvip.edutopia.org/wp-content/uploads/2023/01/PBL_Passion_to_Purpose_Planner-2.pdf

Valenzuela, J. (2023). *Building confident educators.* Edutopia. https://www.edutopia.org/article/confidence-in-teaching

Valenzuela, J. (2024a). *Using instructional rounds to improve learning outcomes.* Edutopia. https://www.edutopia.org/article/using-instructional-rounds-guide-teachers

Valenzuela, J. (2024b). *Creating cohesion among teaching teams*. Edutopia. https://www.edutopia.org/article/building-cohesive-teaching-teams

Van Yperen, N. W., Blaga, M., & Postmes, T. (2015). A meta-analysis of the impact of situationally induced achievement goals on task performance. *Human Performance, 28*(2), 165–182. https://doi.org/10.1080/08959285.2015.1006772

Victoria State Government Department of Education. (2024). *Numeracy for all learners*. https://www.education.vic.gov.au/school/teachers/teachingresources/discipline/maths/Pages/numeracy-for-all-learners.aspx

Wiggins, G., & McTighe, J. (2005). *Understanding by design* (Expanded 2nd ed.). ASCD.

Will, M. (2022). "How bad could it get?" State and district leaders work to combat teacher shortages. *Education Week*. https://www.edweek.org/leadership/how-bad-could-it-get-state-and-district-leaders-work-to-combat-teacher-shortages/2022/03

Wilson, V. (2020). *Creating a culture of professional learning: A practical guide to instructional rounds for educators*. Dave Burgess Consulting, Inc.

The Wing Institute. (2024). *Evidence-based curriculum*. https://www.winginstitute.org/effective-base-instruction-evidence-curriculum

Wong, Z. Y., Liem, G. A. D., Chan, M., & Datu, J. A. D. (2024). Student engagement and its association with academic achievement and subjective well-being: A systematic review and meta-analysis. *Journal of Educational Psychology, 116*(1), 48–75. https://doi.org/10.1037/edu0000833

Woolfolk, A. E., & Hoy, W. K. (1990). Prospective teachers' sense of efficacy and beliefs about control. *Journal of Educational Psychology, 82*(1), 81–91. https://doi.org/10.1037/0022-0663.82.1.81

Wrike Team. (2024). *A guide to writing effective problem statements*. https://www.wrike.com/blog/problem-statement-template/

Zewe, A. (2023). Explained: generative AI. *MIT News*. https://news.mit.edu/2023/explained-generative-ai-1109

Index

Zeitfracht Medien GmbH
Ferdinand-Jühlke-Straße 7
99095 Erfurt, Deutschland
produktsicherheit@kolibri360.de